HOW TO STAY YOUNG

HOW
TO STAY YOUNG

BY
CHRISTIAN D. LARSON

What The Prophet Has Dreamed The Scientist
Will Prove To Be True

New York
THOMAS Y. CROWELL COMPANY
PUBLISHERS

CONTENTS

CONTENTS

HOW TO STAY YOUNG.

INTRODUCTION.

Conclusive Reasons Why Man Should Learn To Stay Young.

The world is changing its thought; in the past, those who believed in the perpetuation of youth were among the isolated few, and were looked upon with suspicion by the many; in the present, the great majority desire to perpetuate their youth, and most of these believe it is possible.

This change of thought is due to two great causes: first, we are fast eliminating the term "impossible" from our vocabulary, and second, we have made several important discoveries in the chemical life—both physical and metaphysical—of the human system.

We are living in an age of wonders, and have come to the conclusion that almost anything is possible, especially if it can add to the welfare, the beauty, the joy and the advancement of human existence.

We are convinced that life is not made for sorrow; we now believe that sorrow is but a temporary creation of man gone astray. We do not believe that this world is a "vale of tears," nor that we must suffer in the present in order that we may gain bliss in the future. We do not gather figs from thistles, neither can a life of pain be the direct cause of a life of pleasure. It is an immutable law that like causes produce like effects, and we are beginning to intelligently use this law in shaping our life and destiny.

The thinking world today is convinced that life is intended by the creator of life to be "a thing of beauty and a joy forever"; we therefore conclude that anything that can add to the joy and the beauty of life must be possible.

That the perpetuation of youth can add to the joy and the beauty of human life is a self-evident fact; and to be consistent in our thinking we must conclude that the perpetuation of youth is possible. An ideal life—the life we picture as the real life—is unthinkable in a world where the age-producing process is constantly at work. To live life as we believe the Creator of life intended life to be lived, this process, therefore, must be removed.

To live as he should live, man must learn to stay young; this is becoming a world-wide conviction, and in consequence thereof, many minds of many modes of research are diligently at work trying to find the great secret of eternal youth.

Many of these are working in the belief that the secret is to be found in the world of material elements, while a constantly growing number are working in the belief that the power of mind alone can perpetuate the youth of the body.

The great facts in nature, however, are never one-sided; they are invariably both physical and meta-physical; they have soul as well as form, spirit as well as substance, and act through physical as well as mental laws.

The secret of eternal youth can not be found through a study of the body alone, nor the mind alone; it does not have its sole existence in the elements of the earth, nor does it exercise its power exclusively through those forces of nature that can not be seen.

That something that produces youth, can, under natural conditions, perpetuate youth; and as this something is an inseparable part of life itself, it can be found only through a study of the process of life as expressed through the whole man. For the same reason, the law through which the perpetuation of youth may be promoted, can be applied only through the living of life as life is intended to be lived.

That something that produces youth, and per-petuates youth, has been discovered; and like all great facts in nature, it is not only very simple, but abides at our very feet. We did not see it, however, because there is a tendency in man to look afar off whenever he is in search of the great and the wonderful. The wonders at his own feet and in his own immediate world are therefore overlooked, at least for a time; but for that something that produces youth the time of enforced seclusion is at an end; it has been found, and is being incorporated as a part of exact science.

The fundamental law through which the perpetua-tion of youth may be promoted is one of the basic laws in nature, and being basic, it is a law that man will not be required to apply; nature already applies this law in the life of man; all that is required of man is to conform the living of his life to this law.

This can readily be accomplished by any person whether he be highly educated, or not; it is therefore evident that anyone can learn to stay young, and there are many conclusive reasons why everybody should learn this most wonderful art.

When we learn to perpetuate youth, we shall add immeasurably to the joy of living, and since man is made for happiness, everything that can increase his happiness should be made a part of his life.

The consciousness of youth will not only deepen and enlarge the consciousness of joy, but the perpetuation of the consciousness of youth will eliminate completely all those ills that come directly from old-age conditions. These ills are almost too numerous to mention, but we can realize at a single moment's thought what a burden will be lifted from the life of the race when complete emancipation from these ills has been secured.

Man would also gain freedom from all these adverse conditions that come indirectly from the aging process; and as these are likewise too numerous to mention, we have another most powerful reason why everybody should learn to stay young.

When great minds come to a place where they have sufficient knowledge and experience to turn their talents to some use that is really worth while, they usually take their departure. But if they knew how to perpetuate their youth, they would not leave this planet just when we needed them the most, and when they could serve us to the greatest advantage.

The great majority of the great minds leave their work upon earth unfinished—not because they have to, but because it is a habit they have inherited from the race; and the loss that the race must annually sustain through the perpetuation of this habit is almost incomprehensible.

The gain that the world will realize when great minds learn to stay young until they have finished their work will be extraordinary, to say the least.

It requires great ideas and great deeds to advance the world; but great ideas spring only from great minds, therefore, great minds should remain upon earth as long as they have something great to do.

It is a self-evident fact that no great mind can be just to himself, to the race, or to the great gifts in his possession, unless he continues to serve the race as long as the race may need him; but to this end he must learn to stay young, and this alone is sufficient reason why he should stay young.

The same is true of lesser minds; when they begin to know enough to live a life worth while on this planet they pass away. While they are mere amateurs on the stage of life they are with us; when they begin to become artists they are with us no more. But it is not right; it means a great loss every day, both to the race in general, and to each individual in particular.

The perpetuation of youth would prevent this loss, and herein we find another conclusive reason why everybody should learn to stay young.

When the average person has gained sufficient knowledge and experience to appreciate the real value of those things that give quality, worth and real joy to life he is too old, too weak or too tired to enjoy them. When his mind is sufficiently developed to partake of the rich feast that the art of man is placing before him, he is too infirm to partake of anything. When he has gained sufficient insight to understand the marvels of nature his senses are dimmed, and the gorgeous splendor of the universe can charm him no more. His loss is great, but if he knew how to stay young his gain could hardly be measured.

If youth could be retained and life prolonged, we should find more time to *Live*, and every moment would be one of contentment and joy. The nervous rush of the strenuous life would cease, because we would realize that there was sufficient time to do everything we wanted to do, and that we could take time to give quality, worth and superiority to every product that was shaped by our hands.

We would not only work for quantity, but also for quality; everything in life would consequently become far richer, and we should also have the time to enjoy this greater richness.

The habit of passing through life in a nervous rush comes originally from the belief that life is so short; we wish to accomplish as much as possible before age and infirmity begin, and rush becomes the order of the day. It is a habit, however, that produces nothing but loss. More mistakes, troubles and ills come from nervous rush than from all other adverse causes combined. The same habit is responsible for a great deal of inferior work, as well as for broken-down human systems.

It is the verdict of exact science that work can harm no one; that it is the nervous rush so frequently associated with work that wrecks the mind and body of man. But this habit will immediately cease when we learn to stay young.

When we realize that youth can be retained for an indefinite period, we shall undertake more, and consequently accomplish more. We shall never fear failure because there will be sufficient time to try again and again until the goal in view has been reached. We shall not, however, become negligent or indifferent, because the life and the vigor of youth will give us ambitions without bounds.

The majority of those who fail, fail because they fear failure, and they fear failure principally because they subconsciously believe the time of action to be limited.

There are very few who undertake as much as they are competent to carry through; and the reason is, they think life is too short in which to complete the greater undertaking.

It is therefore evident that everybody would proceed to do what they were fully competent to do if they knew that they could stay young until their work was finished.

To be just to himself, man must be and do all that he can be and do; but before he will naturally undertake everything that he feels competent to carry through, he must be convinced that he will have sufficient time to complete his work; and this conviction he will gain when he learns to stay young.

To those who desire to develop the greater possibilities that are latent within them, the perpetuation of youth becomes actually indispensable.

To unfold the greatness of mind and soul, the personality must become a more and more perfect instrument of expression; but that personality that is growing older every year is becoming less and less efficient as an instrument of mind and soul. Therefore, those who desire to promote their higher development must learn to stay young.

The most important reason why man should learn to stay young is found in the fact that the perpetuation of youth is in perfect harmony with the purpose of life.

Continuous advancement is the purpose of life; but only those elements in life that stay young can advance. The age-producing process is a deteriorating process, directly opposed to the advancing process. The two, therefore, can not abide in the same person. If the age-producing process continues, advancement will cease, retrogression will begin, and it has been conclusively demonstrated that retrogression, or retarded progress, is the original cause of all the ills in the world.

To promote continuous advancement is to emancipate the individual from the ills that may exist in his system; but to promote continuous advancement it is necessary also to promote the perpetuation of youth; therefore, to secure complete emancipation, man must learn to stay young.

The further development of the faculties and talents of the mind, as well as the functions of the personality, demand the perpetuation of youth. It is not possible to improve that which is growing old, because the age-producing process ossifies, deadens, weakens and deteriorates everything in which it has gained a foothold.

The power of genius demands a young, vigorous personality if it is to give full expression to the highest order of mental brilliancy. It is only a fine instrument that can respond to a fine mind, but to be fine, the instrument must contain the qualities of youth.

The greatest obstacle to extraordinary talent and rare genius is the tendency of the brain to ossify with the passing of the years; and the cause of this tendency is found wholly in the age-producing process. This process, however, will disappear when we learn to stay young.

When we learn to stay young the passing of the years will not decrease the brilliancy of the mind, nor cause the power of genius to wane; instead, every active faculty will become greater and greater the longer we may continue to live.

L

According To Exact Science Man Can Do Whatever He Learns To Do, And He Can Learn Anything.

The nature of man is metaphysical as well as physical; and these two natures are so intertwined that it is not possible to understand the one without understanding the other.

What transpires in the mind will also transpire in the body; and every physical action is both preceded and succeeded by a metaphysical action.

What affects the body affects the mind; what affects the mind affects the body; therefore no final conclusion can be gained concerning any force, action, element or condition in human life unless the factor under consideration is analyzed from the metaphysical as well as the physical point of view.

The facts gained from this mode of analysis constitute exact science, and it is evident, even at a casual glance, that no other mode of analysis can evolve exact science.

Those who have studied only the body do not understand man; and the same is true of those who aim to study only the mind; their conclusions are not scientific, because incomplete; therefore those who act upon such conclusions will fail to secure the desired results.

The principal reason why the secret of eternal youth was not hitherto discovered, is found in the fact that the law through which youth may be perpetuated is metaphysical as well as physical; therefore, neither physical research alone, nor mental research alone could find it.

Another reason is found in the fact that physical science proclaims the limitations of man, and that mental science, by ignoring the true nature of the body, produces limitations in man.

The old thought, whether it be wholly physical or wholly mental, is incapable of giving man the power to do what has not been generally done before; and as the perpetuation of youth is not, as yet, a general accomplishment, a new mode of thought becomes necessary before man can learn to stay young.

This new mode of thought is otherwise termed exact science, and through this science man can learn to stay young, because according to exact science, he can learn anything.

Exact science not only proclaims this as a demonstrated fact, but presents the principles and the laws through which the demonstration becomes possible, no matter by whom these principles and laws may be employed.

The statement that man can do whatever he learns to do, need not be confined to the narrow interpretation of mere objective knowledge coupled with tangible action; it is a statement that will hold true in every form of interpretation, even when considered in connection with the possibility of realizing in the real everything that can be idealized in the ideal.

What man can learn to idealize in the ideal he can learn to realize in the real; this is the conclusion of exact science, and since any desired attainment can be idealized in the ideal, any desired achievement can be realized in the real, because attainments and achievements follow each other invariably as causes and effects.

The fact that the perpetuation of youth can be thought of as an ideal proves that it can be worked out in the real; according to exact science it is not possible to have an ideal until we have the power to make that ideal real.

The reason, however, why the majority who have ideals fail to make them real, is found in the fact that they do not employ the principles of exact science; they depend either solely upon physical laws or solely upon mental laws, not knowing that the nature of man is both physical and metaphysical, and that no change or advancement can be made in human life unless both physical laws and metaphysical laws are employed cooperatively and simultaneously.

The statement that man can learn anything is the logical conclusion of that analysis in exact science that explores the metaphysical as well as the physical. To analyze the mind in its relation to the external world is to find that no limit to the powers of discernment, perception, conception, insight, understanding or comprehension can be found.

A study of the fundamental actions of mind reveal the fact that the more the mind proceeds to learn, the greater becomes its capacity to learn; and as the mind may proceed to learn more and more indefinitely, it may continue to increase its capacity to learn during the same indefinite, or rather, endless period.

To be logical, we must therefore conclude that the mind may learn anything that it proceeds to learn, and that that mind that proceeds to learn everything will constantly be learning everything.

This mode of reasoning, not only proves conclusively that man can learn to stay young, but also that while he is staying young, he can learn everything that may be necessary to make his life as large, as beautiful and as ideal as his soul-inspired heart may desire.

To learn to stay young, and to enjoy in greater and greater measure all the privileges of youth, are therefore possibilities according to exact scientific thinking; but these things are more than possibilities.

A clear understanding of mind reveals the fact that man can learn to do what he has never done before, thus eliminating completely the term "impossibility" from the human domain; the perpetuation of youth, however, has already been done; for that reason it is more than a possibility.

That which has been done once, can be done again, and done better. Every human being has been young, and has stayed young for a time; the law that perpetuates youth is therefore inherent in human nature. What is inherent in human nature can be aroused and employed at any time, and for any length of time; this is natural law, and it proves conclusively that any person, no matter how long he may have lived upon earth, or what his physical condition may be now, can become young now, and can stay young as long as he may desire.

This statement may appear to be too strong, too sweeping, and even unfounded, but no person can analyze the whole nature of man without coming to the same conclusion. It is therefore an indisputable fact, and the truth must be accepted, no matter how much stranger than fiction it may appear to be.

The first essential in learning to stay young is to place the mind in the proper attitude towards the goal in view.

To enter into this attitude it is necessary to establish all thinking upon the conviction that there is no limit to anything in the nature of man; and all thinking must recognize the supremacy of the conscious mind in the life and destiny of the personal man.

It is not possible to become as proficient in any action as one may have the present capacity to become, so long as any form of limitation in human nature is recognized; nor can the individual advance to any considerable degree until all thought of personal limitation is eliminated completely.

The art of staying young is a very high art, and though it is simple when learned, yet it can not be learned so long as the mind has not entered that attitude where it is always at its best. To enter this attitude, and continue in this attitude, all that is necessary is to live in the conviction that the possibilities of human nature have no limitations.

The fact that there are no actual limitations in human nature is conclusively demonstrated by exact science; therefore, any person who will employ the principles of exact science may prove to himself that there are no limitations in his nature. He will thereby become convinced, and will naturally enter the necessary attitude.

To employ the principles of exact science is to analyze everything in human life from the two points of view—the physical and the metaphysical; and those who are not familiar with this mode of analysis will find methods, as well as the detailed application of those methods, in the pages that follow.

The necessity of proper mental attitudes in the perpetuation of youth is clearly evinced by the fact that the personal man is the tangible expression of the mind's subconscious thought, and that subconscious thinking is determined fundamentally by the attitudes of mind.

The personal man is the direct, or indirect result of subconscious thought; subconscious thought is determined by mental attitudes; and man can enter into any mental attitude desired; therefore, any change, modification or condition decided upon may be produced in the personality.

In the last analysis, subconscious thought is fundamental cause of everything that exists or transpires in the personal nature of man; and as man may subconsciously think whatever he desires to think, the nature, the life and the destiny of his personality are in his own hands. That man has the power to perpetuate his youth is therefore a foregone conclusion.

All thinking, however, to produce the desired results, must be consistent with natural law, and must act in harmony with the expression of this law, both in mind and body. To comply with natural law in its physical actions and ignore its metaphysical actions or vice-versa is to neutralize results. The necessity of exact science—the science of the whole man, is therefore evident.

To be consistent with natural law, man must aim to do only that which the laws of his nature make possible now; though all things are possible, still it is the proper application of specific laws that makes them possible.

It would not be possible for man to perpetuate his youth for an indefinite period, if natural law made old age inevitable; nor could man learn to stay young through the application of any other law than the one that produces youth in the domains of nature herself.

Natural law, however, makes no personal condition inevitable; the personality is an instrument, not a final product, and can be changed, modified or perfected to suit the advancing requirements of man.

It is the purpose of natural law to supply man with those essentials that he may require to promote the object of his existence; and as this object is advancement, nature is prepared to supply everything that may be necessary to promote advancement.

The perpetuation of youth is one of these necessities; continuous advancement without continuous youth is unthinkable, a contradiction to every law in human life; nature must therefore have made provisions for the perpetuation of youth. The pages that follow will prove that she has.

To examine man through the principles of exact

science is to find that law in his being that can, will and does perpetuate youth; and since this law is a permanent part of human nature, the finer consciousness of man instinctively feels that youth can be retained.

In every mind where this finer consciousness is recognized and developed, a desire for the perpetuation of youth will arise; whatever we inwardly feel that we can do, we will begin to desire to do, and the more keenly we feel what we can do, the stronger will this desire become.

To discover the purpose of life will also produce a strong desire for the perpetuation of youth, because the finer consciousness in man discerns most clearly that continuous advancement and continuous youth are inseparable factors on the path to the greater life.

It is therefore evident that if man is to do what he is here to do, he must perpetuate his youth; to be true to himself and the life he is here to live, he must learn to stay young.

The coming of man upon earth is not an accident; he is here to fulfill a certain definite purpose, and since continuous advancement in the great eternal now is necessary to promote that purpose, nothing must be permitted in his life that retards advancement.

The age-producing process, however, does retard advancement; to grow old is to go down, to deteriorate, to fail; therefore it is a violation of the laws of life, an obstacle to the purpose of life that must be removed if man is to do what he is created to do.

To be just to himself, man must be now all that

he can be now; he must attain and accomplish all that his present capacity will permit; he must secure from life now all that life can give now; his nature must manifest the highest worth of his conscious being; his world must be filled with the richness of his present sphere of existence; his joy must be complete, and he must *live*.

However, before he can live such a life he must learn to stay young, and exact science declares that he can.

II.

When Man Learns To Be Himself He Will Stay Young Without Trying.

A perpetual renewing process is constantly in action throughout the entire being of man; every cell in the human body is removed after a certain period, and a new one built in its place; this period varies from a few weeks to eight or nine months, at times eleven or twelve months; no part of the human body therefore can be said to be more than a year old at any time.

This fact is one of the most startling as well as one of the most important facts in the science of human life, and it proves conclusively that the age-producing process is an artificial product, placed in action, not by nature, but by the mistakes of man.

To stay young is natural; to grow old is unnatural; therefore, all that man is required to do to stay young is to be natural—to be himself—to be what nature hourly makes him to be.

It is not necessary for man to produce youth in his own system; this is already done by nature; but it is necessary to learn to cease to make the system look old and feel old when it always is young.

To learn to stay young is simply to learn to be what you are; it is therefore one of the simplest arts in the world; there is nothing new to learn, nothing special to do; simply stop doing what you are doing, and leave that which is be what it is.

The fact that the body always is young should cause the body to always look young and feel young; no matter how long the person may have lived upon this planet, his physical form is never more than eight or nine months old, while the greater part of his system has been built up from new material within the last few weeks.

The body of the octogenarian is just as young as the body of the twelve-months old babe; this is a fact in nature—a most astounding fact in the presence of human conditions as we find them.

There is no reason to be found in the domains of nature why the octogenarian should look any older than the twelve-months old child; the fact, however, that the longer people live on earth the older they look and feel proves that some great law in nature is being violated constantly, absolutely and universally.

This great law is the law of perpetual renewal; the law that is constantly rebuilding the human system, removing every fibre in the system after it has been in use for a few weeks or a few months, and causing a new one to be formed in its place.

The new fibres and the new cells are actually new, just as new as the green leaves in the springtime, and when first formed, they are just as new in the body of the octogenarian as in the body of the child. But why are these new cells transformed almost at once into old-looking, weary-looking cells in the body of the octogenarian? This is a question that science must answer, and it is far too important for any form of science to ignore.

The new cells that are formed in the body of the child continue to look new until they are replaced by other new cells; then why should not the new cells in the body of the octogenarian do the same?

In the body of the child the new cells continue young and vigorous so long as they remain in the body, which is but a few months at most; in the body of the octogenarian the new cells wither up, becoming weak and practically useless almost immediately after they have been created; but why? There must be a reason; there is a reason, and exact science has found it.

The law of perpetual renewal does not simply aim to renew the human body; its fundamental aim is to repair and reconstruct the body, and in promoting its process of reconstruction, the process of renewal is promoted through the same action.

The cells and the fibres of the human body are created to perform definite functions, and during the period of their creation are given a certain amount of latent energy; when this energy has all been placed in action, the purpose of the cell has been fulfilled; but instead of recharging that cell, nature removes it as waste matter, and builds a new one, full of youth and vigor, in its place.

This process of reconstruction is constantly in action throughout the human system; the very moment a cell becomes useless, it is removed and a new one built in its place; in a normal human system there is no opportunity therefore, to retain in the system a single cell that is weak, withered or useless.

In a normal human system only young, vigorous cells can remain; when they cease to have life and vigor, they are removed as waste; the fact, therefore, that people who have lived upon earth for a period exceeding thirty or forty years, have withered, useless, empty, old-looking cells in their systems, proves that they are not normal; the law of reconstruction is not permitted to perform its function completely; natural law is being violated and the individual is consequently untrue to himself.

It would not be possible for any person to look old or feel old so long as he was true to himself— so long as he was himself. When man is himself he is young because nature makes him that way; therefore, when man learns to be himself, he will stay young without trying to stay young.

To try to stay young is to fail to stay young. To try to be what you already are is to proceed in the belief that you are not what you are; you will thereby misdirect your energies, and consequently fail to reach your goal.

When man discovers himself, and learns to be himself, he will discern the *modus operandi* of his real nature; he will discern that his entire system is constantly being renewed, and will cease to interfere with the renewing process; instead, he will feel that he always is young, and his desire to express what he is will perpetually increase.

The more perfectly the mind discerns its own true nature, and the more keenly the individual be-

comes conscious of his complete self, the stronger becomes the desire to perpetuate the qualities of youth.
The reason why is found in the fact that the more
perfect conscious realization of self will place the
mind in more perfect contact with the fundamental
law of self, and will consequently desire more and
more to act in harmony with this law.

To act in harmony with the fundamental law of
self is to be oneself, and to be oneself is to be young
because nature is perpetually making the self young.

That nature is ever making the self young through
the law of repair and reconstruction can be demonstrated conclusively by any chemist; and every close
student of human life knows that the very moment
the process of reconstruction should cease, all conscious life would depart from the personality.

When the cells of the body have served their purpose they become mere waste matter, and as no cell
in the body can continue in action more than a few
months, the entire body would, in a few months be
a mass of waste matter if the process of reconstruction
were suspended.

The process of reconstruction, however, in order
to perpetuate the life of the body, removes every cell
after it has remained in the body for a few months,
and forms a new one in its place. The entire system,
therefore, is being perpetually renewed; in fact the
human personality must continue absolutely in the
hands of the law of reconstruction and perpetual renewal to live a single day.

The human personality has been placed permanently in the hands of this law, and will remain per-

manently in the hands of this law, or until man so
completely violates this law that he severs his connection with personal existence.

The fact, therefore, that the human personality
is completely governed, and perpetuated in its existence by the law of perpetual renewal, proves that it
is being perpetually renewed, and is always young.

The very moment the personality ceases to be renewed, it will cease to exist as an organized form;
the continuation of organized life demands the continuation of reconstruction, and reconstruction means
renewal—the perpetuation of youth.

A closer study of the law of reconstruction reveals the fact that nearly ninety percent of the cells
in the average human body are replaced by new cells
in less than four months. Those muscles that are
exercised to a considerable degree every day are completely renewed every three, four or five weeks, depending upon the nature of the exercise and the health
and vigor of the body.

To promote the orderly renewal of the muscles,
the best exercise is that which never goes beyond
moderation and that is never mechanical. Mere mechanical exercise will weaken the muscles, while violent and too constant exercise will destroy many of
the cells that are still new and vigorous.

The purpose of physical exercise is to place in
constructive action all the energy generated in the
system; and when all of this energy is in constructive
action, the entire personality will renew itself orderly,
rapidly, completely and perfectly. It is therefore evi-

dent that forced action or retarded action will interfere with the work of the reconstructive process.

The average athlete grows old rapidly and dies young; the reason being that his exercise has been too violent, or too mechanical, or both.

Those muscles that are called into play during work that is thoroughly interesting, receive the best exercise, and therefore will renew themselves most thoroughly in the least time.

All muscles, however, are renewed, whether they are fully exercised or not, but where the exercise is very slight, the old cells may remain nearly a year before they are replaced with new ones.

The vital organs, such as the heart, stomach, lungs, etc., renew themselves rapidly, providing the health of the body is reasonably good.

The average person who breathes properly and breathes only pure air, will receive three pair of new lungs every year.

When the stomach is never overloaded nor abused, it will renew itself from two to three times every year; the same is true of the other organs in the abdominal region.

The heart, the arterial system, the brain and the nervous system will, under normal conditions, renew themselves every sixty or ninety days, while the skin is renewed completely every week or ten days.

The bony structure of the human body requires the longest time to complete the renewal process, the time required, varying from seven months to a year, at rare intervals, fourteen months.

When the health of the body is not perfect, the

renewal process is somewhat retarded, but even chronic invalids will renew their bodies completely in less than a year and a half.

In the face of these facts, where does old age have an opportunity to present itself? This process of renewal is constant, and will continue, with but slight variations, so long as the personality continues to live. The entire human body is therefore always young, and for that reason should always continue to look young and feel young.

The fact that the body, after leaving the teens, does not look as young as it actually is, proves, as stated before, that some natural law has been violated.

To cease to violate this law, and to learn to live in perfect harmony with this law, is all that is necessary in order to stay young; mere simplicity itself when accomplished, but before it can be accomplished, the ordinary mode of living and thinking will have to be reversed.

To begin, the individual must learn to be himself; he must learn, not only to think of himself as young, but to *Be* young, because he is young. The actions of thought, feeling and consciousness must reproduce in the mental life, as well as the personal life, the same qualities of youth that nature is producing in the chemical life.

The movements of man himself must produce youth, and reproduce youth, thus cooperating with the renewing process everywhere in action among the movements of nature.

The real life of man is young at all times, and everything that lives in the being of man, is, for the same reason, young at all times. Therefore, to be young, man must live his real life; he must not live an artificial life, nor live in an artificial mental state. He must be himself, and live in the conscious realization of what he is in the reality of himself.

Youth is not merely skin deep; it is the result of an interior life-process that penetrates every atom in the being of man, and gives eternal youth to every atom in the being of man. No external lotion will therefore produce the qualities of youth, neither will chemicals, externally or internally applied, count for anything whatever.

The secret is to enter into the consciousness of this interior life-process; and it is in this consciousness that man enters when he is himself.

Youth comes from within; it already exists within the life of every fibre in the human system, but man, through the violation of certain laws, prevents the youth within from coming forth into full and natural expression.

To promote the full and natural expression of youth, man must be himself; he must be young in thought, life and consciousness because he is young in himself; and to train the mind to be young, the fact that the entire human system is being renewed perpetually should be constantly impressed upon the mind.

The individual should train himself to live in the constant recognition of the great fact that his body is always young; that every fibre in his being is now as new as the leaves and the flowers of the springtime; and that every fibre will, in a few short weeks, be replaced by another, fresh from the hands of creative power.

To train the mind to constantly recognize the perpetual youth of the body will cause consciousness to enter more and more deeply into that interior life-process that always is young, and that causes every atom in the being of man to always stay young.

To live in this consciousness is to discern the actions of the law of perpetual renewal; and to discern this law is to discard everything in thought or action that violates this law.

When the law of perpetual renewal is no longer violated, the body will always look and feel as young as it is; and as the body always is young, the individual will continue to look young and feel young, no matter how long he may continue to live upon this planet.

This may appear to be a far-reaching statement, but it is the conclusion of exact science, and as exact science is based upon absolute facts as they stand in the complete nature of man—physical and meta-physical, to be true to the truth, there is no other alternative than to accept the statement, and act accordingly.

It is the truth that the personality of man is always young; therefore when man permits himself to be himself he will always stay young without trying to stay young.

III.

Why Man Looks Old Though Nature Gives Him A New Body Every Year.

There are two reasons why the personal man, after reaching what is termed middle life, begins to look older and older in appearance every year. The one is ossification and the other is old-age conditions.

The tendency of the human body to ossify is produced by various causes, some physical and some mental, though all of these causes, in their last analysis, have their origin in certain abnormal modes of mental life.

When the cells and the fibres of the body begin to ossify, the muscles will harden, the bones will become stiff, the various organs will become heavy and sluggish, and a shriveling up process will pervade, more and more, the entire system. Reconstruction and repair will be retarded, waste matter will increase in the system and will soon begin to clog the system because the various organs are too sluggish to perform their functions properly.

When the cells of the brain begin to ossify, they will respond less and less to the actions of the mind; the intellect will become less and less lucid, and memory will gradually wane. New impressions are formed in mind with difficulty, usually not at all; the acquisition of new knowledge becomes almost im-

(29)

possible as the brain is no longer a perfect, responsive instrument upon which the mental faculties may act.

The fact that "old people" remember more readily what occurred in their childhood than what occurred in recent years, is in this connection, simply explained. The impressions formed upon the mind in childhood were deep and penetrating because the brain was then in a plastic condition; later impressions, however, scarcely produced any impression because the brain had become too hard; that the impressions gained in childhood should be vivid while the impressions of recent years are hardly perceptible is therefore evident.

The same phenomena explains why a number of "old people" who have left the beliefs of childhood, return to those beliefs in their "declining" years. When the brain becomes so ossified that clear, penetrating, comprehensive thinking becomes difficult, or impossible, the mind can discern only those ideas that are deeply impressed, and naturally can believe only that which it can discern. And as the deepest impressions are always those impressions that are formed in childhood, that is, in the minds of those who permit ossification to take place, the beliefs of childhood are the only beliefs that "old" ossified brains can understand.

The fact that "old people" frequently return to their earlier ideas proves nothing for or against those ideas; it only proves that ossified brains are too dull to discern other than the deepest impressions in the mind; and those impressions are usually the ones gained in childhood.

When the "old people" become childish, the cause is the same; their brains are too dull to be influenced by the wiser ideas of later years; such brains discern only the deep impressions of childhood, and are influenced by the nature of those impressions, and consequently become childish both in thought and action.

The impressions of childhood are not always the deepest and most vivid impressions, however; if the brain is just as plastic at sixty as at ten, the impressions formed at the one period may be just as deep as at the other; but in the average person the brain begins to ossify at fifty, sometimes at forty or thirty-five.

Minds that are highly developed will form their deepest impressions after the half-century mark has been passed, providing the ossifying process does not enter the brain. It is therefore evident that those minds that are constantly being developed, and that never permit the brain to ossify will do their best work later in life; in fact, the nearer they approach the century mark the more remarkable will their work become.

The fact that ossification can be prevented, not only in the brain, but in the entire human system, is therefore tidings of great joy, especially to those who wish to live a life worth while and accomplish something worth while.

The second reason why man looks old though nature gives him a new body every year, is found in old-age conditions. These conditions are purely mental and are produced principally by the conscious or subconscious belief in age.

To believe that you are growing older and older every year, and to positively expect to look older and older every year, is to produce old-age conditions in the system; these conditions will cause the new cells that have just been formed, to take on an old-age appearance, and thus the new body will look as old as you think you are, regardless of the fact that the new body has been in existence less than a year.

The old-age conditions will bear the stamp of your thought of yourself, because they are the product of your thought of yourself; therefore, if you have lived upon this planet for fifty years and think that you ought to look just as fifty-year-old people are supposed to look, you will create old-age conditions that have the fifty-year-old stamp, and your new body will be stamped by this old stamp.

The new body will be so permeated with fifty-year-old conditions that it will feel like fifty and look like fifty. It is all false, however; there is not a cell or a fibre in your system that is over a year old; the majority are less than three months old, therefore, could not look as if they were fifty unless they were changed artificially by some false mental process.

The fact that the actions of the mind can change the appearance of the body is thoroughly demonstrated whenever a person worries or indulges in similar mental states. A few hours of worry will cause the person to look ten, and even twenty years older than he did before the worry began. Then what may we not expect from a lifetime of constant old-age producing thought?

The power of thought is creative, and the conditions that are produced by thought are similar to the nature of the thought itself; therefore, to constantly think, year after year, that you are growing older and older, is to fill the system with conditions that will impress the appearance of more and more age upon every fibre and cell in the system.

The new cells that are formed in your body today will be caused, by these old-age conditions, to look as old as you think you are today; next year you will think you are a year older, and the old age conditions that are constantly being evolved from your mentality, will cause you to feel a year older, and the entire body to look a year older.

To think that you are growing older, or to expect to grow old some time in the future, is to form old-age conditions in the mentality; therefore, no thought whatever must be given to old age, or the age-producing process in any of its forms.

The chemical processes of the body, the vital processes of the functional system, the conscious processes of the brain and nervous system—in brief, all the processes of the personality, obey the ruling tendency of the mind absolutely; the mind can, either through direct or indirect action, modify all the natural processes in the human system; the process that perpetuates youth can be neutralized by the adverse actions of the mind, and this is what the average mind is doing; to learn to stay young, therefore, it is necessary to change the mind completely on this most important subject.

The color of the hair changes with the passing of the years because it is a race habit to grow gray as you are growing old. It is a tendency that every person inherits from the race, but the time of its action varies among different persons to a considerable degree. This variation is produced principally by personal habits and environments, and occasionally by exceptional conditions in mind or body.

The tendency to change the color of the hair was originally produced by adverse mental states, the result of which was intensified by repetition. The longer the person lived, the more he worried, the more he grieved, and the more he misdirected the efforts of mind, thought or action; and as these continued to change the color of the hair more and more, man came to look upon the change as the result of age. Finally it became a race habit, but it is well to remember that all habits can be removed.

To dwell a great deal in wrong mental states will tend to change the color of the hair before the race tendency we have inherited begins to produce the change; and to continue to dwell in wrong mental states after this tendency has begun to act, will increase the power of this tendency. This is why some people grow gray early in life, and why others grow gray very rapidly when they once begin.

In the presence of the fact that the entire body is constantly renewed, it seems difficult for some minds to understand why scars, tumors, artificial growths, etc., continue to appear in the same place, and frequently in the same form, year after year; but this is a matter that is simply explained.

Every cell in the human body is produced by an individual chemical action, and this action has its root in the subconscious life of the body; to change the form or the nature of the cell this chemical action must first be changed, and this is possible through the use of any method that will effect the subconscious root, or cause of that action.

It is possible, however, not only to change the subconscious cause of any chemical action along the line of orderly development, but it is also possible to produce unnatural chemical actions. This frequently occurs both through external agencies and through conditions that arise wholly within the system itself.

When any part of the body is cut, the chemical actions within the cells that are affected, are so shocked that they become unnatural actions. These unnatural actions will tend to produce cell structures similar to the cut through which they had their origin; that is, they will tend to produce and perpetuate a scar.

Nature, however, always aims to remove unnatural chemical actions, and when it succeeds the scar finally disappears. Sometimes it succeeds only in modifying the false action, while at other times it fails, the reason being that the unnatural chemical action has become so thoroughly individualized and so firmly established that nature can not remove it without assistance.

Artificial growths in the body are produced by unnatural chemical actions that have become individualized. These particular actions usually have their origin in diseased conditions within the system, and they will continue to produce the artificial growth until nature can remove them. If nature fails, other agencies, either physical or metaphysical, will be required to reestablish normal conditions.

The fact that every chemical action, both natural and unnatural, has its origin in the subconscious life, gives extreme importance to that phase of metaphysics through which the subconscious may be changed and reconstructed in any manner desired. Since the subconscious can do whatever it is properly directed to do, any false chemical action, and in consequence, any artificial growth in the system, can be removed by those who know how to direct the subconscious.

The law of perpetual renewal will renew all the cells in the system, whether these cells are the expressions of natural chemical actions or not; but the new cells will, in each case, have the same form and nature as the old ones, because the same causes always produce the same effects.

An artificial growth in the system will renew itself just as rapidly as any organ in the system, but the new cells in the artificial growth will be similar to the old ones because they were all produced by the same unnatural chemical action.

An artificial growth that is growing will multiply cell structures through the same law that multiplies cell structures in a growing muscle, but each individual cell will be similar to the cell that preceded so long as the individual chemical actions remain unchanged. When these actions change, the efforts of nature, singly or in cooperation with external assistance, are responsible.

To those who understand the nature of the human organism, it is evident that the law of perpetual renewal is ceaselessly at work rebuilding everything, both the natural and the unnatural, in the personality of man; everything in the human system is always new, therefore should never look old, and never would look old if ossification and old-age conditions were not produced in the being of man.

Nature, however, does not produce these two causes of the aging process; they are both produced by the mistakes of man, and he himself can completely remove them.

When man removes the process of ossification from his physical system, and removes every age-producing thought from his mental system, he will have mastered the art of staying young.

Great minds have for some time realized that the perpetuation of youth would be possible if ossification could be overcome, and have searched diligently for that strange chemical action that, seemingly without reason, hardens the cells of the system with the passing of the years.

Their failure to find it, however, is due wholly to the fact that we can not understand the secret processes of life until chemistry is combined with metaphysics.

The cause of ossification is partly physical, partly mental and partly hereditary, and these various phases of the subject will be analyzed thoroughly in succeeding chapters; but in our effort to remove the process of ossification, we must not forget to hold the mind in that attitude where old-age conditions of thought are eliminated completely.

It will not be possible for man to perpetuate his youth, no matter what methods he may employ, so long as he believes in the reality and the inevitableness of age. To live in the belief that age must come is to mentally create the age-producing process, or to perpetuate the age-producing process that we have inherited from the race. And to create or perpetuate that process is to fill the system with old-age conditions, and we will look as old as we think we are, regardless of the fact that our present body has been in existence but a few short months.

To fix a future time for the coming of age, is to impress the idea of age upon the mind, and to impress the idea of age upon the mind is to impress conditions of age upon the cells of the body.

We are receiving from nature perpetual youth now; to live in that youth now is to retain that youth now; and as there is no end to the eternal now there can be no end to the youth of the eternal now.

The future will care for itself if we care well for the present, and to be true to the present we must be true to ourselves in the present; we must be what we are now, and we are young now.

To think, at any time, of the possibility of future age is to create age-producing thought; it is to create that thought now that has no place in life now; it is to bring age into the present when there is no age in the present.

The present body is young; it is this year's product; it is new and ought to look new; but man thinks he is old because he has lived upon earth sixty or more years; he therefore feels as old as people are supposed to feel at sixty, and the body always looks as old as the mind feels.

The body always is young, and will look young as long as the mind feels young; this is the great secret.

IV.

Growing Old Is A Race Habit That Can Be Removed.

The scientific analysis of the subconscious mentality of the human race proves conclusively that the tendency to grow old is a mere habit. It is a habit, however, that has been acquired by the race as a whole, and is therefore transmitted to every child coming into the world.

Through the force of this habit we all think subconsciously that we are growing old, that age is inevitable, and that nothing can prevent the final culmination of age. We think these thoughts without knowing what we are doing, because that mode of thinking has become a part of the subconscious life. But by this mode of thinking we constantly direct the subconscious mind to produce the conditions of age, and whatever the subconscious is constantly directed to do, that it constantly will do.

The cause of every habit is found in some subconscious action, and whenever any subconscious action becomes fully individualized it acts automatically when prompted to do so, either by its own inherent tendency or by the influence of corresponding suggestions from without.

To individualize a subconscious action is to form a habit, and every conscious action that is frequently

(40)

repeated will become an individualized subconscious action.

There are a number of conscious actions that tend to produce age, and many of these have been repeated so constantly, and for so many ages, by the individuals of the race, that they have become individualized subconscious actions, that is, race habits.

The habit of growing old was therefore originally produced by the repetition of those conscious actions that tend to produce age; in like manner, the habit of staying young may be produced by frequent repetitions of those conscious actions that tend to promote the perpetuation of youth; and as every habit may be removed by establishing an opposite subconscious tendency in its place, the possibility of removing the growing old habit is positively assured.

The subconscious mind can be entirely changed and completely reconstructed in all its phases, and since every habit is subconscious it is evident that every habit can be removed.

The fact that the tendency to grow old is a race habit proves that no person can stay young simply by accepting the idea that he naturally is young. Though nature gives him a new body every year, the growing old habit causes that new body to look old and feel old; therefore, if the new body is to look young and feel young, the growing old habit must be completely removed from the subconscious mind.

To remove this habit it is necessary not only to change the subconscious mind in this respect, but also necessary to change the conscious ideas of everything we see in tangible life.

The entire human race is growing old because every child was born with the habit; therefore the idea of age is constantly being suggested to our minds, and this idea is constantly adding life to the growing old habit. To prevent this we must constantly impress upon our minds the fact that the tendency to stay young is alone natural.

The tendency to imitate the false must be counteracted by training our minds to think and act in perfect harmony with the law that produces perpetual youth.

The conscious conception of life must be formed in the exact likeness of the absolute truth about life, and according to absolute truth, that is, exact science, man never grows old. He may change his youth into age through the violation of natural law, just as he may change the conditions of his physical system from health to disease through the violation of natural law, but it is only through the violation of natural law that age and disease can come. While man continues to be true to himself he is always well and always young.

To remove any race habit, it is necessary to act upon the fact that it is only subconscious tendencies that are inherited. Man does not inherit disease, or weakness, or adverse characteristics; but he may inherit the subconscious causes of these conditions.

Therefore, to prevent the mistakes of the race from being reproduced in ourselves, it is necessary to eliminate from our subconscious minds those adverse tendencies that we may have inherited from the race. The tendency to grow old is one of these, and it may be removed by training the subconscious mind to work in harmony with the natural renewing process.

It is not possible, however, for the conscious mind to direct the subconscious to work in harmony with the natural renewing process, so long as the idea of old age is believed to be real.

What we think of as real we impress upon the subconscious, and what we impress upon the subconscious, is seed sown in the garden of life; it will invariably bear fruit after its kind.

The idea of the three score and ten must be forgotten, and the idea that life can perpetuate youth so long as you may desire youth, must be impressed upon the subconscious instead.

The fact that the mistakes of man made the three score and ten practically the limit of his physical existence, originated the belief that the three score and ten was the natural limit, and that a longer life was merely accidental. But that which is produced by the mistakes of man does not corroborate what is produced by the laws of nature.

The laws of nature declare that there is no limit to the possibilities of life; neither is life confined to certain special actions. It is just as easy for the forces of being to perpetuate youth as to produce age; it requires no more energy to do the one than the other, but what these forces are to do man himself must determine.

It requires no more life-force to live a thousand years than to live one day; the living of life does not exhaust life, but rather develops the power of life. It is the misuse of life that alone will exhaust life;

therefore, when man learns to live life he will no longer be limited in any form whatever, by those conditions that have sprung from the mistakes of man.

To continue to believe that certain things must be because they have been, is to place the mind in complete bondage to the habits of the race, regardless of the nature of those habits, whether they be detrimental or not.

We are not required to believe anything but the truth, we are not required to do anything but that which promotes the highest welfare of each and all; and it is the understanding of life itself that reveals what thought to think and what action to pursue.

To continue to grow old simply because the whole race is growing old, is not scientific; the free mind refuses to grow old unless nature says he must. And to the mind that is free, free from race thought, free to think the truth as it is, nature declares that to be true to himself he must stay young.

The average mind is practically filled with adverse tendencies and habits that have been inherited from the race; these tendencies are implicitly obeyed by the forces of the system, because these forces are controlled by the subconscious, and the subconscious always does what it has been directed to do.

It is therefore evident that the average person is doing a great many things, not because they are right and natural, but because he has inherited the habit from the race. And since the majority of the race habits originated in the prehistoric mistakes of man, the present man to be just to himself, must examine his life anew. He must no longer continue to do

things because they have been done; his purpose,
henceforth, must be to learn what his life actually is,
and act accordingly.

What a man thinks is of extreme importance, because what he thinks or believes with conviction will
impress the subconscious, and what the subconscious
is impressed to do it invariably will do.

To believe that you will finally grow old is a
habit; every child is born with the cause of that belief
in its mind; but that belief will daily impress the subconscious to produce age, and age will be produced.

To believe that you are young now, and that nature is giving you a new body now, may be simple if
your present body looks young and feels young; but
in the midst of the realization of present youth, nearly
every mind will persist in believing that age will come
sometime. This belief, however, must be eliminated
completely, and the subconscious mind must be trained
to think the truth about life as it is.

To believe the truth about yourself is to believe
that you are always young, because the law that perpetuates youth can not cease to perpetuate youth so
long as life has personal existence.

To believe with conviction that you are always
young is to impress the subconscious with the idea
of perpetual youth, and accordingly, the subconscious
will begin to produce the elements of youth. The
habit of growing old will cease and the habit of staying young will be established in its place.

The fact is that however long you may live in
your present organized form, you will have a new
body every eight or ten months. This body ought

to look new, and would look new if the subconscious system had not inherited the habit of growing old. The personal man should look young and feel young, at all times, regardless of the years.

It is not the truth that years produce the feeling of age or the appearance of age; years produce experience, and experience, if not misapplied, will develop both mind and body. Development, however, means improvement, but it is not possible for that to improve, that is growing old and useless, neither is it possible for that to grow old and useless that is constantly being improved.

It is the truth that not a single cell in the human system ever becomes old; the belief in old eyes, therefore, is a false belief.

The belief that the eyes need glasses when they become "old" is a race habit, and it is contrary to every fact in exact science. The eyes do not become old; there is not a human eye on the face of this planet that has been in existence more than six or seven months; the same is true of all the other senses, and the fact proves conclusively that the only reason why the eyes become weak and dim after a certain number of years, is because the subconscious system has formed that habit.

To think that your eyes are growing old and dim is to impress age and weakness upon the subconscious life of the eyes, and according to subconscious law, conditions of age and weakness will be formed in the eyes. The eyes will consequently feel old and weak, not because they are old and weak, but because they are filled with weak, old age conditions

Where the eyes are defective in shape, glasses may be used to advantage for the purpose of correcting the defect, but this use should be temporary only, and should be taken up with that thought in mind.

No person should ever begin to wear glasses in the belief that he will have to use them all his life, nor should anyone ever think that his eyes will need glasses when they become old, because the eyes do not become old.

To live in the belief, however, that the eyes will grow old is to fill the eyes with old age conditions, and as such conditions interfere with natural functions they are invariably weakening in their effect.

The eyes of the octogenarian are no older than the eyes of the seven year old child; the eyes of both persons have been formed within the last six or eight months, and, therefore, the one pair is no more in need of glasses than the other.

The belief that the bones must become stiff, the physical organs weakened, the memory impaired, etc., when "advanced age" has been reached, is likewise contrary to exact science. There is not a single cell in the human system that will have to ossify, no matter how long the person may live.

The ossifying tendency is also a race habit, but like all other habits, it can be removed completely.

All the signs of "old age" are abnormal, produced by subconscious tendencies or habits that each individual has inherited from the race; no mind therefore, to be truthful, can speak of age as being natural and inevitable, nor can any person be true to himself unless he removes all age producing tendencies from his system absolutely.

To try to demonstrate, in detail, that the tendency to grow old is a mere race habit will not be necessary, because the fact proves itself so completely the very moment the true relationship between physical conditions and subconscious actions is discerned. It is the removing of this habit, however, that demands our best and most thorough attention.

To proceed, the first essential is to remove the age producing tendency from the subconscious, and the second is to train the conscious mind to think the exact truth concerning the appearance of old age conditions.

When conditions of age are in evidence anywhere in our environments, the conscious mind should impress upon itself the fact that there is only eternal youth in the true state of life. All conditions of old age should be looked upon as unnatural, and every idea of old age should be contradicted at once.

The conscious mind should think of old age as contrary to nature, as a mere race habit, for which no individual is directly to blame, and should think of the age producing process as something that any person can eliminate from his system at will.

What enters the mind through the senses will impress itself upon the mind, and will tend to reproduce itself in the life of the individual; for this reason, the idea of age must never enter the mind, and all thought of age should be immediately dismissed as unreal, the very moment it is suggested to consciousness.

The conscious mind must look upon old age conditions as foreign, as wholly false, and as things apart from the real life of man. No attempt, however, should be made to resist these conditions, because they have neither power nor existence of their own; they simply are creations of our own minds, and will cease to be when we create them no more.

To remove those subconscious tendencies that cause the creation of old-age conditions, it is necessary to form mental tendencies that are directly opposite in nature and purpose; the principle being that no mental state or tendency can be removed unless it is displaced by its exact opposite. The darkness disappears only when displaced by the light.

The habit of growing old will disappear when we form the habit of staying young, and to the art of forming this habit a separate chapter will be devoted.

When the tendency to grow old is recognized as a race habit having its origin in the prehistoric mistakes of man, we may be tempted to think that the habit is too well established to be removed in our own lifetime; we may argue that what is a race habit can only be removed by centuries of training in the formation of the opposite tendency, and that that training will have to be applied to the entire race.

Such conclusions, however, are not scientific; it is not necessary for the entire race to learn to stay young before individuals may acquire that art, any more than it is necessary for the entire race to develop genius before we may have genius in the individual. Besides, man will not be required to produce youth; he already is young; he will simply have to remove the habit of growing old, and this any individual can do now.

All habits are subconscious, and anything can be removed from the subconscious by anyone at any time.

The subconscious can do and will do whatever it is directed to do, and it begins to act the very moment the directions are being made. It is therefore in the power of every individual to learn to stay young now.

V.

Eliminate The Consciousness Of Age By Living In The Great Eternal Now.

The forces of the mind will create and express every quality or condition that is held in consciousness. This is one of the most important of all metaphysical laws, because it is principally through this law that man determines what his personal life is to be.

To live in the consciousness of age, is to create in mind the conditions of age, and what is created in mind will invariably be expressed in the personality. Therefore the consciousness of age must be eliminated completely before the perpetuation of youth can be promoted.

The consciousness of age is produced by the belief that time is passing and that the longer man continues to pass with time the older he becomes.

This belief, however, is a direct contradiction to the facts of exact science; first, because time does not pass, time *is;* and second, because the perpetual renewing process, inherent in man, prevents him from growing old no matter how long he may live.

The true conception of time is extremely important in placing the mind in the proper attitude towards the laws that govern the being of man; and this true conception is based upon the principle that time *is.* Time neither comes nor goes; it is the movements of **nature** that come and go, not time.

What we call time is but the *now* of eternity, **and** this now is eternally in the now; therefore there **can** be no passing of time.

It is only in the now that man can live; he **can** live neither in the past nor in the future; he **may** think of the past or the future, but he can live only in the now. And since the now does not pass, the life of man does not pass.

When man believes that many years constitute age, and that the passing of time produces the many years, he will unconsciously live in the feeling that he is growing older and older with the passing of the years. He will feel older and older every year, and the body always looks as old as the mind feels.

However, when man realizes that many years do not constitute age, and that the years do not pass, he will no longer feel that he is growing old, and consequently will no longer look old.

To train the mind to concentrate the whole of attention upon the great eternal now is to develop the consciousness of the "isness" of the now, and to consciously feel that the now *is*, is to eliminate the consciousness of age completely.

It is not possible for the mind to feel that it is growing old so long as it feels that it lives in the now, and that the now *is*.

The now is eternal; that is, the now eternally is now; the now never ceases to be now; therefore to *live* in the now is to continue to be now what you are now, and you are young now.

It is possible for man to grow and develop in the now, but he will never pass out of the now, because the now is eternal.

Man should affirm to himself "I am not passing with time, because time does not pass; time *is*. I am living in the now, and the now continues eternally to be the now. I am living and growing now, but I am not passing towards age. There is no age, and I do not pass; I am."

When man develops the "I Am" consciousness, he will attain the realization of what he is now; he will discern that his present nature is limitless in possibility, and that the conscious possession of more and more of the richness of his nature will come, not from more and more years of development, but from more and more present realization.

He will discern that he may accomplish whatever he has in mind by perpetually increasing his present realization of what is latent in his nature now. He will not look to the future for greater attainments, but to the growth of the present, and will consequently concentrate the whole of attention upon the now.

To live in the realization of the now, with no direct thought of the past or the future, is to eliminate from mind the "passing of time" attitude; and when this attitude is removed the consciousness of age will disappear completely.

When man is no longer conscious of age, he will no longer create old age conditions, and therefore, will permit his system to be what nature makes it to be now—young.

To perpetuate the youth that nature is producing

now, live in the eternal now, and know that you are
young now. Know that the youth producing process
in your system is as eternal as the now, and that you
therefore will always be young no matter how long
you may live.

To live in the great eternal now is to give the whole
of attention to the work of the present moment; it is
to recognize neither past nor future; it is to think
neither of what has been nor what is to be; it is to
live, think and act only for what can be lived, thought
and attained now.

To live in the great eternal now, is to act upon
the principle that it is only what we do now that
determines results. The past is gone; it concerns us
no more; and since the future will be the natural out-
come of the present, the more perfectly we live for the
present the greater will the future be.

To live in the great eternal now, is to be so completely absorbed in the now that there is consciousness neither of the past nor the future; the only consciousness is the consciousness of the now.

To live in the great eternal now, is to realize that
there is no past, that there is no future; all is now,
because the now always *is* now, always was now, and
always shall be now.

There is no time but the now; and the now does
not pass away; therefore there is no passing of time;
all time is, and in that time man always is.

The heavenly bodies, in their movements, do not
record the passing of time, neither do they measure
time; they simply record their own speed as they
move in the great eternal now; they simply measure

the changing distances between their own changing positions as they move about the great center of life during the great eternal now.

The universe is not passing away; some parts are only moving around other parts and these parts are moving around still other parts that in turn move around something else; all is motion, but all motion is in circles. The universe is eternally where it is, eternally moving in circles where it is, thoroughly and eternally alive, and all taking place during the great eternal now.

Everything is for the now because the only time that is, is now. Man is conscious only of the now, and to look into the depths of the now is to find that everything is contained in the now.

To give the whole of attention to the now is the secret of gaining in the now all that man may want now. That which is not done for the now is scattered, and will either be wasted entirely or will produce results that are detrimental to man's welfare now. It is only what is done for the now that adds to man's welfare now, and when man lives, thinks and acts exclusively for the now, his life will be complete now.

To live in the great eternal now, is therefore the only scientific mode of living, whatever the individual viewpoint of life may be; and it is one of the fundamental essentials in the art of staying young.

To live in the great eternal now, fix no special time for anything in the future. Plan for the future when such plans are necessary to the promotion of what you are doing now, but consciously *live* in the now.

No thought should be given to what may happen

in the future; such thought is wasted because we can not deal with that which is not here. All the power of life and thought should be used in causing the best things possible to happen now. Such action will not only improve the present, but will also train the mind to eliminate the consciousness of age by giving the whole of consciousness to the now, where age is not.

Learn to be more now, develop yourself now, promote your growth now, and you will become more and more competent to deal with that which may transpire in your life. You will gain the power to make the future far better than the present; you will feel the constant increase of this power and will therefore have no anxiety about the days that are to be.

To make the best of the present is to make the future better, but to make the best of the present all life, all thought and all action must be concentrated absolutely upon the present; no thought must be given to the future; in fact, so completely must attention be concentrated upon the work of the present that we are unconscious of everything but what we are doing now.

To think of the future is to think of how long we may live, and how many years we shall pass through before we reach the expected goal. Such thought will cause the mind to feel that time is passing and that we are passing with time into weakness and age. The consciousness of age will thus be produced, and to be conscious of age is to produce the conditions of age in our own systems.

The great question with man is not how long he may live in any particular sphere of existence, but how well he may live where he is living now; and he who lives well where he lives now will live a long time where he lives now; that is, if he so desires.

The man who lives well while upon earth will live a long time upon earth, and retain his youth as long as he lives.

To live well, however, it is necessary to live absolutely for the great eternal now; to live now the life of youth now; to be conscious only of the now, and to realize that both the now and the youth that is produced now are eternal.

To realize that man is eternal is to eliminate the subconscious feeling that we are passing towards that condition of age that is supposed to be in store for every person in the future; and to realize that the youth of the now is eternal is to eliminate the consciousness of age, thus removing the principal cause of old age conditions.

The fact that nature is perpetually renewing the entire being of man, proves that there is no condition of age in the future towards which man is supposed to pass; such a belief is a mere illusion, because the only age that appears in the human system is the age that man himself produces through the violation of the laws of life.

To avoid the violation of these laws it becomes absolutely necessary to live, think and act only for the great eternal now. Everything that is done should be done "just for today," and the ruling purpose of life should be to live today the greatest life that is possible today.

The object is to eliminate the consciousness of age,

because when man is no longer conscious of growing old he will cease to grow old. The new body that nature is constantly producing in man, will stay new when man ceases to make that which is new look old and feel old; instead, he will look young and feel young; and it is natural that he should, because he is young.

To eliminate the consciousness of age the principal essential is to realize that time is; that time is not passing, and that therefore man is not passing with time.

The feeling that we are growing old is produced by the belief that every year adds so much to the age of man; but the facts of exact science prove that the years do not produce age; also, that nothing but the violation of law can produce age.

The consciousness of age is therefore the consciousness of abnormal conditions, conditions that have been produced, not by nature, but by the mistakes of man; and these conditions can be removed only by the development of that consciousness that is absolutely normal, based upon the realization of what is true in the real life of nature.

The first essential in the development of normal consciousness is to place the mind in contact with the present natural processes in the human system. The most important of these are the process of perpetual renewal and the process of present creation.

The first of these rebuilds the entire human system during every period of eight or ten months, thus keeping the body forever young.

The second process creates in the system all those

conditions or qualities of which the mind is conscious; but its work is of, for, by and through the present only.

To place the mind in contact with this second process is to prove to the mind that there is no other time in nature but the now, and that there is no other action in nature but the action of the now. And when this fact is proven to the mind, the whole of attention will naturally be directed absolutely upon the time of the now and the action of the now.

In this manner, natural consciousness will be developed, because the more the mind associates with the true processes of nature, the more keenly will the mind feel that which is natural; and since it is natural to live for the now, the mind will, through the development of natural consciousness, enter absolutely into the life of the now.

To live absolutely in the life of the now is to be conscious only of what is true in nature now; and it is true in nature now that man is young now.

It is therefore evident that man will continue to stay young so long as he continues to live absolutely in the great eternal now.

VI.

Training the Subsconscious to Produce Perpetually the Elements of Youth.

The subconscious mind has the power to keep the body in health, youth and vigor for *any length of time.*

The subconscious mind is the source of every quality, condition, characteristic, tendency, desire, element or power that appears in the human personality; and as a source it is inexhaustible; therefore, when man learns to draw upon his subconscious source, he may increase any power, perpetuate any condition, or perfect any quality to the highest imaginable degree.

The subconscious can do and will do whatever it is properly impressed or directed to do; it is therefore evident that any person may, through the proper direction of his subconscious mind, produce youth in his system now, and perpetuate that youth for as long a time as he may desire.

Whatever the present condition of the body may be, the subconscious can remove that condition so that the new body that nature has recently produced may appear as it is—full of health, youth and vigor.

The subconscious mind is the inner side of the whole mind of man; the conscious mind is the outer side. The conscious mind is the wide-awake mind,

the subconscious is the interior depths of mentality.
The conscious mind is the thinker, the subconscious
is the doer. The conscious mind gives directions, the
subconscious carries them out. The conscious mind
is the sower, the subconscious is the mental soil—inexhaustible in the richness of its productive power.

The ideas, the thoughts, the beliefs, the desires
and the aims of the conscious mind are mental seeds,
and when these are deeply felt they will enter the subconscious, invariably producing fruits after their kind.

To train the subconscious to produce the elements of youth, only those ideas, thoughts, beliefs and
desires should be entertained in the conscious mind
that are conducive to youth and perpetuation of
youth. .

It is not possible for any state, condition, element
or power to be expressed in the human personality
until its cause has been formed in the subconscious.
All causes are held and worked out in the subconscious. The conscious mind originates the cause, the
subconscious takes it within itself and evolves the
natural effect.

All causes are subconscious, and all subconscious
causes bring forth their effects into the outer mind
and body. Therefore, the subconscious cause of youth
must be established before youth will express itself
in the personality.

The subconscious mind of the child contains the
active cause of youth, and also the inactive, latent
cause of old age. The former cause is produced by
the natural renewing process, and so long as this cause
is permitted to act, youth will appear in the person-

ality. The latter cause is inherited from the race; it is the age producing race habit, and according to the tendencies of its own inherent nature, will begin to produce the old-age condition at the expiration of a period of thirty, forty or fifty years.

To perpetuate youth it is therefore necessary to remove the subconscious age-producing cause that has been inherited from the race; and to remove this cause the entire subconscious mind must be trained to produce perpetually the elements of youth.

All age-producing causes will disappear from the subconscious when the entire subconscious mind is permeated with youth-producing causes, and this is our object in view.

To promote this object, the conscious mind must proceed systematically and thoroughly to re-create the subconscious in all its phases; the subconscious must be directed to do everything that is necessary to produce and perpetuate youth, and every subconscious tendency to the contrary, must be displaced by a youth-producing tendency.

To proceed, the subconscious should daily be impressed with the fact that you are young now. What you impress upon the subconscious, the subconscious will express in mind and body; therefore, when the subconscious is deeply and thoroughly impressed with the fact that you are young now, it will produce and express throughout your system the elements of youth now. You will consequently feel young and look young, and you should, because you are young.

When the subconscious is impressed with the fact that you are young now, it will cease to follow the race tendency to interfere with the natural renewing process, but will instead, work in harmony with this process, thus removing from the system every age-producing habit or tendency that has been inherited from the race.

To impress the subconscious with the idea that you are young now is not to present to the inner mind some imaginary idea; you are young now; it is no theory; your entire system has been made new within the last few months; therefore, permeate your mind through and through with the very spirit of that great truth.

To try to impress an idea upon the subconscious that you know to be untrue is to fail; the subconscious will only accept those ideas that you inwardly feel to be absolutely true.

The subconscious will not obey the doubting mind, but the mind of faith and conviction can make the subconscious do anything within its power to do, and

To try to impress an idea upon the subconscious there are no limitations, neither is there any end.

To live in the conviction that you are young now is to constantly direct the subconscious to make you look young now, feel young now, and express, through and through your system the vigor of youth now.

The subconscious can; the subconscious can do and will do whatever it is properly directed to do.

What the subconscious has been properly and thoroughly trained to do it will continue to do for an indefinite period, or until the conscious mind gives directions to the contrary. Therefore, when the subconscious has been trained to produce the elements of youth, it will continue to produce these elements per-petually, thus insuring continuous youth for that individual so long as he may live upon this plane.

When the subconscious mind has been trained to produce perpetually the elements of youth, it will not only produce these elements in its own person-ality, but will transmit the youth-producing tendency to the next generation.

When both parents have eliminated from their subconscious minds the age-producng race habit, and have permanently established instead the subconscious youth-producing process, their children will be born absolutely free from the age-producing habit of the race.

Such children will not be born with the habit of growing old, but will be born with a strong subconsci-ous tendency to stay young as long as they may live. Such children will never grow old unless they acquire the habit, later on in life, through the misuse of their own minds.

To transmit to their children the perpetual youth producing tendency, it is necessary for the parents, however, to permanently establish this tendency in their own subconscious minds before the conceptions of those children are to take place.

It is the law that whatever the parents have estab-lished in their own subconscious minds, they will transmit to their children; the possibilities of parent-hood are therefore immeasurable, and to those who understand the unfoldment of these possibilities, than parenthood there is no greater greatness.

The subconscious minds of all persons, whether

they be octogenarians, or in their teens, contain the age-producing tendency; young parents will therefore transmit this growing-old race habit to their children just as readily as those parents that have begun to show the signs of age; for this reason, all persons who expect to become parents must completely remove this race habit from their subconscious minds before they can transmit the youth-producing tendency to their children.

Those parents who succeed only partly in removing the age-producing process from their systems, will give their children the power to retain the vigor of youth for a longer period than the average; but all parents can succeed completely in this respect, and all should proceed with that determination in mind.

Every effort to direct the subconscious to do what we desire to have done, should be promoted in the firm conviction that the subconscious can. To have absolute faith in the subconscious is to reach the inexhaustible powers of the subconscious, and when these powers are reached there is no object in view that can not be accomplished.

To properly impress any idea or desire upon the subconscious, the conscious mind must not only be firmly convinced that the idea is true, but must keenly feel the nature and the purpose of that idea; and there is no attitude of mind that will promote these two essentials as thoroughly as faith. Every effort therefore that is made in the training of the subconscious should be permeated with strong invincible faith.

The fact that the body is being constantly renewed makes it possible for the subconscious, not only to perpetuate the elements of youth in the body, but also to constantly improve everything in the human personality.

Therefore, when the subconscious is being directed to produce the elements of youth, it should also be directed to produce the elements of beauty and physical perfection. Impress upon the subconscious the most perfect idea of physical beauty that the mind can possibly conceive, and desire with deep feeling, that the elements of that beauty be produced and expressed through every atom of the physical form.

In like manner, direct the subconscious to build for yourself a finer and a finer personality, a stronger character and a more brilliant mind. And always proceed in the faith that the subconscious can.

Whenever you think of yourself, mentally see yourself as the picture of health, youth and vigor, and introduce into that picture the most perfect idea of physical beauty that you can possibly imagine.

This picture should be daily impressed upon the subconscious; that is, while holding the picture in mind, think of the subconscious with deep feeling, and try to feel that the elements of the picture are being appropriated by the subconscious.

Every mental picture that is properly impressed upon the subconscious will be reproduced in the human system, because whatever is impressed upon the subconscious will be developed and expressed in the personality.

To mentally live in the world of this picture will aid remarkably in bringing the nature of the picture into the subconscious, and this is especially true when the mind pictures itself in the world of health and youth.

To mentally live in a certain state or attitude is to take that state or attitude into the subconscious. That which we *live* we invariably impress upon the subconscious; therefore to perpetually live in the spirit of youth is to cause the subconscious to perpetually create the elements of youth.

To live in the belief that you are growing older every year is to direct the subconscious to make you feel older and look older every year; and this is what nearly every person is doing, though principally through the force of habit—race habit. He is thereby training his subconscious mind to produce old age; but it is just as easy for the subconscious to produce perpetual youth if properly directed to do so.

When the subconscious is trained to produce youth, and express youth throughout the entire personality, it will cease to produce conditions of old age, and will consequently interfere no more with the perpetual renewing process; instead, it will promote that process.

To remove the tendency of the hair to change its color at those periods when race thought expects it to change, direct the subconscious to perpetuate the natural color of the hair.

The fact that the color of the hair has already

begun to turn gray need not cause anyone to hesitate
to apply this method. The actions of the mind *can*
produce chemical changes in the physical system; to
restore the natural coloring matter of the hair would
be no more difficult for nature than the healing of a
wound; but changes and modifications in human nature can be produced only through the subconscious,
therefore, the subconscious must first be directed to
do what we wish to have done.

To direct the subconscious to perpetuate the natural color of the hair, picture this color as clearly as
possible in mind; then, with deep feeling, impress the
soul of this picture upon the subconscious; that is,
place your thought in the very soul, or inner life of
that color, and impress that thought upon the depths
of subconscious life.

To mentally live in the absolute faith that the subconscious is perpetuating the natural color of the hair
is sufficient where the color has not begun to change;
but where the change has begun, special attention must
be given to the matter daily to restore normal conditions.

To retain the natural color of the hair it is also
necessary to avoid strenuous mental action, hard
thinking, forced thinking, nervousness, worry, fear and
similar adverse mental states.

This is also true with regard to the perpetuation
of youth throughout the system; all mental states
must be harmonious, and all physical conditions
wholesome.

To secure harmonious mental states and wholesome physical conditions, all that is necessary is to

direct the subconscious to produce them; the subconscious can.

To direct or impress the subconscious with the
positive assurance of securing the desired results, there
are three fundamental essentials to be closely observed. First, the idea to be impressed should be
clearly discerned in mind; second, when concentrating
this idea upon the subconscious, the mind should act
in the attitude of the deepest possible feeling; and
third, the real existence of the subconscious mind
itself should be felt in every part of the personality.

The subconscious mind occupies the entire personality and fills every atom with its finer mental life;
in fact, it is an immense, inner, mental world that
permeates every part of the being of man; therefore,
when trying to impress an idea upon the subconscious,
attention should be concentrated upon the finer life
that permeates the outer life.

When the conscious mind *feels* the finer life of the
subconscious mind, the thought of the conscious mind
is in contact with the power of the subconscious, and
whatever the conscious mind, during this contact, may
desire to have done, the subconscious will proceed to
do.

This contact is always produced when the conscious mind is in an attitude of deep feeling, and this
deep feeling will invariably follow the combined action
of faith and desire—the desire to impress the subconscious, and the absolute faith that the subconscious
can do whatever it is impressed to do.

VII.

Conscious Harmony with the Law of Perpetual Renewal.

The entire universe is perpetually passing through a process of renewal; nothing is fixed; all is change, and the purpose of this change is to make all things new at all times. Every action in nature tends to counteract permanency or age, and every movement in life has youth and progress in view.

All things live, move and have their being in the spirit of change, and this change is produced by the law of perpetual renewal, a law that underlies everything, permeates everything and acts through everything.

This law is perpetually at work through the human system, changing everything, renewing everything, but what the results of this change are to be in the life of the individual depends upon how he relates himself to the law that produces the change, and how fully he cooperates with the original purpose of that law.

When the mind acts in conscious harmony with the law of renewal, the results of that law will be expressed through the life, the mentality and the personality of the individual; but when the mind fails to act in harmony with that law these results will be neutralized.

(70)

The law of renewal makes all things new at all times in the entire human system, but whether the new system is to express new conditions or continue to express old conditions will depend upon whether or no the results of the law of renewal are neutralized by the human mind.

The mind of the individual can permit the new fibres and conditions of its own system to appear new, or it can cause the new to look old and act as if it were old; that is, the mind can give full expression to the results of the law of renewal, or it can completely neutralize these results.

When the mind places itself in harmony with the law of renewal, and recognizes its existence at all times, every action of the mind will become a renewing process, and will cooperate with the law; in consequence, that which is renewed by the law of renewal will be expressed through mind and body in its original newness; it will not be changed, colored or modified by mental interference as it is being expressed, but will come forth as it is—absolutely new.

When the mind does not act in conscious harmony with the law of renewal, and does not recognize the existence of the renewing process, every action of the mind will tend to reproduce the old. As the new is coming forth, fresh from the law of renewal, the mind will cause it to be reproduced in the exact likeness of the old; the results of the renewing process will thereby be neutralized, and though everything in the system continues to be renewed, nothing appears as if it were renewed.

When the mind acts in ignorance of, or at variance

with, the law of renewal, it follows the groove of the age-producing race habit, and causes what has been renewed in its own system, to be changed so that it looks old, feels old and acts as if it were old.

The mind acts in every atom of the being of man, and has the power to change, color or modify whatever is taking place in the human system; what is changed by the mind becomes more or less similar to the predominating thought, feeling or condition of the mind; therefore, what is renewed by the law of renewal will become old in its nature so long as the mind feels old, acts as if it were old, and believes that all things are growing old.

The mental forces are creative but they invariably create in the exact likeness of the predominating ideas, beliefs, feelings or attitudes of mind.

When the mind feels old, the creative forces will cause everything in the system to look as old as the mind feels; and the mind that is ignorant of the law of perpetual renewal will feel older every year because it believes that all things are growing older every year.

The mind that acts in conscious harmony with the law of perpetual renewal will *feel* that all things are new now, and in consequence, the creative forces of the system will give newness, youth and vigor to everything in mind or body.

To train the mind to act in conscious harmony with the law of perpetual renewal, the existence of this law, in every part of the system, must be recognized in every thought, feeling or attitude. Every trace of belief in age or the aging process must be eliminated completely, and the fact that all things are new now must become a firm conviction.

The mind must aim to perpetually renew itself, and this aim may be promoted by training every process of thinking to form new thought, better thought, greater thought and superior thought about everything that enters consciousness.

The thought of today, on every subject, must be new as compared with the thought of yesterday, and every idea formed in mind must be an improvement upon the corresponding idea that was formed before.

Every mental conception that is formed today, on any subject, should be finer, higher and superior to the previous conception formed on the same subject.

To constantly renew its own thinking, and improve its own thinking should be the ruling purpose of mind, and the highest possible point of view should be taken in mind at all times, whatever the subject of thought may be.

The mind that is perpetually renewing itself will think new thought and superior thought on all subjects at all times. Such a mind will comply with one of the greatest of all statements in exact science, "Be ye therefore transformed by the renewal of your mind," and will, in consequence, not only realize perpetual youth in the physical system, but will also transform, advance and perfect the entire world of mind and character.

To continue the thinking of "old thought" is to perpetuate those hereditary tendencies that produce the aging process, because old thought is thought that does not change or improve. New thought produces new life, more life and greater life, while old thought weakens, deteriorates and ossifies the entire system.

That which is perpetually renewed will never weaken, unless the results of the renewing process are neutralized; but these results can only be neutralized by the mind that lives in the non-progressive attitude of old thought; this attitude will disappear, however, when the mind begins to perpetually renew itself through the thinking of new thought—thought that is always renewing itself by constantly improving upon itself.

When the mind dwells in the old thought attitude, the renewing process will fail to cause the new to be different from the old, but when the mind is constantly breaking bounds, constantly moving forward into the new, the superior and the greater, the renewing process will invariably cause all things in the human system to become, not only new in appearance, but superior in expression and greater in action.

The law of perpetual renewal will cause everything to improve as it is being renewed, providing the mind lives in conscious harmony with the law of renewal by constantly renewing itself.

The perpetual renewal of mind is readily promoted when consciousness is placed in perfect touch with the spirit of change that pervades all things; and that this spirit does pervade all things is clearly discerned when the mind is placed in harmony with the real life of nature.

The entire universe is in perpetual motion, and since motion invariably produces change, everything in the universe is passing through perpetual change.

Change implies renewal, therefore the fact that nature does supply the law of perpetual renewal is demonstrated conclusively.

This law is constantly remaking everything; all things are ever new and ever becoming new; all things therefore should appear new, that is, under normal conditions; but the fact that the new seldom appears new in the being of man, proves that he is not living under normal conditions.

To produce normal conditions man must live a normal life, and to live a normal life is to live in harmony with the fundamental laws of nature. One of the most important of these is the law of perpetual renewal; therefore every mind that does not aim to promote perpetual renewal is not living in harmony with nature.

The mind that is not living in harmony with nature is producing abnormal conditions, and it is such conditions that change or neutralize the results of the renewing process, thereby causing the new to appear as if it were not new.

That which is normal is never old; it is normal or natural to be new and young at all times, because one of the principal laws in nature is ever making all things new.

Those conditions that appear to be old are abnormal; all appearance of age is artificial, and comes from the race habit of mentally interfering with the law of renewal.

The workings of nature do not produce the conditions of age; such conditions are produced by man's failure to work with the renewing process of nature.

All conditions of age, and all the results of what man calls age are unnatural, and must disappear when man becomes natural.

To be natural is to live, think and act in conscious harmony with the purpose of nature, and this purpose is to renew everything and improve everything in the being of man.

The fact that nature has provided the law of perpetual renewal, and based everything upon this law, makes it unnecessary for man to try to change; he already *is* changing; what man is required to do is to cease to resist that change, and to cease to pervert the results of that change.

Man is not required to produce perpetual renewal in his system, but to train himself to live, think and act in conscious harmony with that perpetual renewal that is already taking place.

The law of perpetual renewal is producing perpetual youth in the human system, but the results of this law are modified to such an extent by the false actions of the mind, that the new body does not look new, nor feel new, but looks and feels as old as the mind thinks it now is according to race belief.

To remove these false actions of mind so that the new body may look as new and feel as new as it actually is, this is the object in view; and when this object is fulfilled, man will look young, feel young and stay young as long as he may live upon this planet.

To remove any false action the opposite true action must be established in its place; to prevent the mind from interfering with the process of renewal, all the forces of mind must be trained to promote that renewal, and to train the mental forces in this respect all thinking must become, in itself, a renewing process as well as a developing process.

To perpetually renew itself, the fundamental aim of thinking must be the formation of higher and higher conceptions concerning everything that may be discerned by consciousness.

When the mind begins to think, its aim should be to think better thought, larger thought and greater thought; and the desire to improve constantly upon all previous thought should be made so strong that all the elements of mind are drawn into the very spirit of that desire.

To increase the power of this desire is to cause all the forces of mind to work for the purpose of this desire; and when this is accomplished, the tendency to renew itself and improve itself will become so strong in the mind, that every process of thought will become an improvement of thought.

To think is to think better—that will be the condition of such a mind, because every mental action will have formed the inherent tendency to renew itself and improve itself whenever it is placed in action.

When the mind has established this mode of thinking it will renew itself constantly, and will consequently act in conscious harmony with the law of perpetual renewal. Instead of neutralizing the results of this law, the mind will fully express these results. The new body will look new, feel new, and express all the power and vigor of youth. The personality will continue to stay young, because the new body that nature is giving to man every year, will be burdened no more with old age conditions.

It is the mind that lives in old thought that fills the new body with old age conditions, thus causing the new to look old and feel old; but when the mind begins to renew itself perpetually there will be no more old thought nor old age conditions; old age will vanish like a dream, and man will continue to stay young as long as he remains upon this planet.

VIII.

Why Experience Produces Age when Its Real Purpose Is to Perpetuate Youth.

To live is to think; to think is to act, and to act is to produce experience; experience must therefore invariably follow the expression of every process in life.

To live is to live more, because living produces experience, and experience opens the mind to the newer, the larger and the greater.

To gain experience is to gain wisdom, power and a larger field of conscious action; and since the enlargement of the field of conscious action is the direct cause of the renewal of mind, the perpetual renewal of mind must invariably follow the perpetual gain of experience.

The gain of experience, however, is continuous, because while life continues, the gain of experience will continue.

The perpetual renewal of mind will perpetuate the youth of the entire personality; and since the inherent tendency of experience is to renew the mind, the real purpose of experience must be to perpetuate youth.

To perpetuate youth in the complete sense, is to promote the growth, the development and the advancement of everything in the being of man, and to gain experience is to gain the elements of advancement;

(79)

therefore, the tendency of experience is inseparably connected with the tendency of life to advance itself, renew itself and perpetuate its own youth.

To live is to gain experience; to gain experience is to gain the power to live more, and to live more is to perpetuate youth. It is not possible to grow old while life is on the increase.

The gain of experience will produce two opposing tendencies in mind, depending upon the use that is made of the mental elements produced by the experience. The one is a tendency towards the feeling of maturity, the other is a tendency towards the feeling of conscious expansion.

When the mind thinks of development as a process having a definite end in view, the mental elements produced by experience will be used for the purpose of bringing this end into realization; and as this end is being approached the mind feels that it is being matured.

The feeling of maturity tends to retard further advancement, because further advancement is not supposed to be possible where maturity has taken place. Therefore, the mind that permits the feeling of maturity to act in the system will cause a maturing process to be placed in action throughout the system, and as the maturing process is gaining ground, the advancing process is losing ground.

The gradual suspension of growth in one part after the other will be the result, and that which ceases to grow will begin to grow old.

When the mind thinks of development as being perpetual, there will be no thought of any end; every step in advance will be looked upon as a step towards more advancement; the feeling of maturity will therefore be eliminated completely.

To think of every experience as being an open door to a larger mental world is to cause every experience to produce the feeling of conscious expansion, and what the mind feels it is doing it is doing.

The inherent purpose of every experience is to produce conscious expansion, and so long as this expansion is perpetual the renewal of mind will be perpetual; in consequence, youth will be perpetual; but this inherent purpose of experience is interfered with by the process of maturity.

The maturing process, however, is not natural; it is the result of wrong states of mind, being a direct contradiction of the growing process which is natural.

The maturing process has an end in view, and intends to cease action when that end is reached; the growing process has no end in view, and does not intend to cease action at any time. The growing process does not think of the finished product; it simply thinks of growing now, therefore, perpetuates the force of growth now.

In the true order of things, nothing is ever finished; what seems to be finished is but an introduction to something still greater that is to follow, and the process of growth works ceaselessly through all these stages of advancement.

It is therefore evident that to think of maturity and expect maturity, is to introduce a false process in the human system, and as this maturing process does have a tendency to retard natural growth it will prevent the natural renewing process of the system from perpetuating the youth of the body.

The reason why experience tends to produce age in the average person is, according to this analysis, clearly discerned in the fact that the race lives in the belief that experience produces mental maturity; and since the condition of maturity suspends growth, age must follow, because that which ceases to grow begins to grow old.

The condition of age is simply a condition of retarded or suspended growth; it is a condition wherein development has ceased, and wherein retrogression and decay have begun, or are about to begin. But it is not possible, however, for retrogression or decay to take place anywhere in the system so long as growth, development and advancement are in action.

Where progression is in action, retrogression is impossible, and where there is growth, there can be no decay; therefore, the promotion of uninterrupted growth and continuous advancement in the human system will eliminate every condition of age; in consequence, youth will be perpetual.

The law of perpetual renewal provides for continuous growth and advancement in every part of the system, and experience opens the mind to larger fields of action, thereby giving the process of growth the opportunity to promote the development of the human system on an ever-enlarging scale.

In this plan there is no place given to the aging process, therefore, the aging process will never enter the system unless it is produced by man himself through the violation of these fundamental laws in nature.

The inherent purpose of experience is expressed through one of the most important of these laws, and to comply with this law, the mind should be trained to act in harmony with the purpose of experience.

This may be accomplished by causing the conscious mind to think of every experience as a path to greater things, and by causing the subconscious mind to *feel* the expanding, growing, advancing tendency of every experience.

The subconscious mind should be daily impressed with the fact that every experience has an expanding, growing, advancing tendency; ere long this inner purpose of experience will be subconsciously felt, and thereafter the subconscious mind will act in harmony with the tendency of experience.

The conscious mind should expect every experience to open the way to the new, and should confidently live in the very soul of that expectation. In consequence, all the forces and faculties of the conscious mind will move with the tendency of experience—the tendency to enter the new—and will, thereby, constantly enter the new.

When the conscious mind is ever entering the new, and the subconscious mind is constantly acting in harmony with the expanding, advancing tendency, the perpetual renewing process will be promoted throughout the entire personality. The perpetuation of youth must invariably follow, because every condition of maturity and suspended growth will entirely disappear.

When the mind feels the conditions of maturity, these conditions will be expressed in every part of the system, especially in the face, where the expressions of mind are the strongest, and conditions of maturity invariably produce the appearance of age.

It is therefore evident that the unnatural tendency to mature is one of the principal causes of the aging process.

The growing mind, however, does not mature; the more the growing mind develops the more it finds to develop, and the stronger becomes its desire to work out the new possibilities that are constantly being discovered. Such a mind never feels matured nor gives expression to maturity; nor can anything come to a standstill and ossify in the personality of such a mind.

The average person, after having passed through a great deal of experience, feels old and worn, because he has looked upon experience as a wearing process instead of as a process of renewal, growth and advancement. In consequence, he looks old and worn, and is gradually placing his entire system under the complete influence of the aging process.

Experience implies action, and action, as ordinarily expressed uses up energy; therefore it is believed that much experience will produce a worn, wearied condition. But the ordinary expression of action does not apply the true purpose of action; results—worn and wearied conditions are for that reason abnormal.

The true purpose of action is to place in action more and more of the stored up energy of the system; and as experience tends to enlarge the sphere of action, it is a foregone conclusion that experience, when not interfered with, will invigorate both mind and body.

When each action in the human system tends to place more stored-up energy in action, the power and the capacity of the system will naturally increase, and such results may be secured from every action when the mind is trained to think of every action, not as a wearing process, but as a building process.

To train the mind to use every experience, that is, every group of new actions for the purpose of awakening potential power, is to promote the real purpose of experience, because the perpetual renewal of the entire system demands a constant increase in the expression of life.

To train the mind for this purpose, every experience should be consciously used as a path to the newer, the larger and the greater.

The mind must be trained to think, both consciously and subconsciously, of every experience as an open door to a new world. To enter this door whenever it opens, is to perpetually renew and enlarge the mental world, and while the mental world is being perpetually renewed, old age is impossible.

When the mind thinks of every experience as a developing and enlarging process, there will be no tendency in experience to produce conditions of maturity or age, but every experience will be left free to promote its own inherent purpose, which is to perpetuate the new by ever and ever opening the mind to the new.

The action of every experience tends to produce an impression upon the mind, and the result of this impression will depend upon the mental attitude towards experience while the impression was being made.

To form these impressions with the greatest of care is highly important because these impressions determine the nature of thought, and man is as he thinks.

Those impressions that are fixed in their nature will tend to produce stationary conditions in the system and such conditions invariably become old-age conditions. Impressions, however, that are created with an inherent desire to reproduce themselves and enlarge themselves, will originate advancing thought; that is, thought that will work in harmony with the natural renewing process, and thus perpetuate the elements of youth.

To simply "pass through" experience is to impress consciousness with the idea of wear and tear, and this idea, as it forms itself into conditions, will age the personality.

When passing through experience, the mind should aim to "pass out" of the experience that is produced by experience; this effort will impress consciousness with the idea of advancement, and advancing ideas are always rejuvenating.

To pass out of experience while passing through experience is to increase the power of the ascending tendency of thought, and such thought not only perpetuates youth but also develops the faculties of the mind.

To think of every experience as a passing out of the lesser into the greater, is the accurate thought to form concerning the nature, the tendency and the purpose of experience.

There must be no settling down into grooves; nor must any one think that he is entitled to fixed ideas and final conclusions because he has had an abundance of experience.

There are no final conclusions; every demonstrated fact simply demonstrates the fact that every fact begins to evolve into new and different facts the very moment it has passed through its demonstration.

There are no fixed ideas; an idea to be an idea must be a growing idea. What we call fixed ideas are simply ossified thoughts; they are not alive, therefore, have no truth in them.

The mind that has had an abundance of experience should know that he has just begun to deal with real ideas; that there are universes before him still to be explored and comprehended, and that the experience he has had thus far is mere insignificance compared with what is yet in store for advancing human thought.

To gain these greater ideas man must enter into harmony with the real purpose of experience, and begin to live solely for continuous advancement. While so living he will also perpetuate his youth.

IX.

All Thinking Should Animate the Mind and Invigorate the Body.

The forces of thought have the power to affect, not only the personal appearance of man, but also the chemical elements of his system. To retain his youth, man must therefore educate himself to think only those thoughts that have a youth producing tendency.

To think old thought is to give the personality the appearance of age, and all thought is old thought that is not inspired by the spirit of growth and progression.

To think heavy thought is to depress the entire nervous system; and a burdened nervous system tends to produce heavy, depressing conditions in every cell in the body. These conditions, on account of their chemical weight, will tend to harden and ossify the cell structure, and as a result we have conditions of old age.

To think new thought is to give the personality the appearance of youth, and all thought is new thought that is created by the forces of mental expansion and growth.

To think new thought is to cause all thinking to act in harmony with the law of perpetual renewal; to think old thought is to cause all thinking to interfere with this law; it is therefore clearly discerned how

(88)

old thought tends to produce old age, while new thought tends to perpetuate youth.

To think new thought is to cause all thinking to animate the mind and invigorate the body; but new thought is not a system of ideas; *new thought is the latest product of a growing mind.*

When the mind accepts a system of ideas, it ceases to think new thought, and begins to think old thought. The creation of old-age conditions will inevitably follow.

To think new thought at all times, the mind must expand and develop at all times; it must ascend and break bounds, not only once, but constantly. It is only the growing mind that thinks new thought, and it is only the man who is forever thinking new thought who can stay young.

To think new thought, all thinking must be expansive, and every mental action must aim to enter a larger field of action. This will cause the mind to constantly renew itself and enlarge itself, and the conscious possession of more life and power will follow.

To increase the conscious possession of life and power, is to re-animate the mind and re-invigorate the body, and while the mind is being re-animated and the body re-invigorated, the aging process cannot possibly gain a foothold in the system.

In the average mind there is a tendency to think old thought, and to make all thinking hard and heavy. The tendency to think old thought comes from the race-habit of permitting every idea that is accepted to remain in the mind unchanged. It becomes a mental fixture, and continues to inspire the same kind of thinking over and over again, year in and year out.

This is the origin of stereotyped thinking; such thinking produces old thought, that is, thought that never changes; and old thought produces old age.

To remove the tendency to think old thought, the mind should aim to develop, enlarge and perfect every idea that may be accepted, and should work in the conviction that every idea does contain unlimited possibilities.

To eliminate hard and heavy thinking, the usual methods of thought, research and mental penetration must be replaced by methods that are in harmony with natural mental expansion.

The cause of hard and heavy thinking comes principally from trying to find the solutions for the larger problems of life by searching in the present limitations, present incompleteness, or present darkness of the mind.

The mind can not understand the larger while confined in present limitations; to try to do so would result in hard and heavy thinking. Such efforts would weary the mind, and nearly all mental weariness or exhaustion is produced·in this way.

When the mind is in a state of clouded or incomplete intelligence, no effort should be made to understand facts, principles or problems that can only be discerned through the light of a brilliant intelligence; such efforts will not only produce hard, heavy thinking, but the mind will be confused and darkened more than it ever has been before.

The proper course to pursue is to increase the

brilliancy of the mind; to make the mental light stronger; when this is done the mind can readily see what it desires to see.

There is practically nothing that the mind can not discern in its present sphere of existence when intelligence is sufficiently brilliant; but when intelligence is not sufficiently brilliant, it can not fully understand anything it may desire to understand, no matter how hard and persevering its efforts may be.

To understand what we desire to understand, the secret is not to try to force the mind into the necessary sphere of comprehension; in fact, we should never "try hard" to understand anything, but should simply proceed to "turn on" more mental light.

To increase the light, the intelligence and the brilliancy of the mind is to give the mind the power to see and understand whatever may be at hand, without the slightest mental effort.

To understand the principles of life, to penetrate the mysterious phases of life, and to solve the everyday problems of existence, the secret is simply to turn on more mental light.

That which seems mysterious, seems so because there is not enough light; mystery and darkness always go hand in hand. Remove the darkness, and the mystery is no more.

The human mind is constituted so that it can clearly understand anything that may enter its mental world, providing there is enough mental light. Therefore, to turn on the necessary mental light is not only to eliminate ignorance and mistakes, but hard and heavy thinking as well.

To increase the light of the mind, the actions of consciousness should break bounds, and place themselves in touch with the universal. No direct effort should be made to understand what may be under consideration until the mind has first illuminated itself.

The mind that is illuminated can understand without trying to understand; such a mind can see more, it can see further, and it can see more clearly.

The illuminated mind can learn easily and rapidly; no strained effort is required, and no hard mental work; it is in the light, therefore can readily see whatever it may desire to see.

The art of learning, not through hard, strenuous, wearisome study, but through the scientific illumination of the mind, is one of the greatest secrets in the new psychology, and should be taught to every child. We should thereby give mental brilliancy and remarkable talents to the great majority, and hard thinking, one of the principal causes of old age, would be removed completely.

The scientific illumination of the mind may be brought about, first, by recognizing the fact that every mind lives and moves and has its being in a universal sea of absolute intelligence, and second, by training the mind to consciously *use* absolute intelligence in every process of thinking.

There is only one power of intelligence in the universe, and each individual mind employs as much of that one intelligence as its present conscious capacity can appropriate; but that capacity can be constantly increased, and as it is increased, the individual mind gains conscious possession of more intelligence; that is, more light is turned on in the mind.

When the mind places itself in perfect conscious touch with absolute intelligence, it responds to the greater power of that supreme intelligence in which it lives, acts and thinks, and will consequently use as great a degree of absolute intelligence as consciousness can comprehend at the time.

The degree of intelligence that is employed by the mind when it responds to absolute intelligence is always far greater than that which the mind employs when conscious only of its own limited objective mentality; and this is the reason why the mind always outdoes itself when it transcends itself.

To recognize the fact that the individual mind is an expression of the absolute mind, and that the intelligence of the individual mind increases as its conscious unity with the absolute mind is realized, is to place the individual mind in harmony with the power of absolute intelligence; and when this harmony is established, the power of absolute intelligence will begin to work through the individual mind.

The power of absolute intelligence, however, is not a power outside of and distinct from the individual mind; it is the same intelligence that is in action in the individual mind, only in a much lesser degree.

When the individual mind begins to respond to absolute intelligence, it does not receive a different form of intelligence compared with what it now has, neither does it admit an outside power to come in and think in its stead; the individual mind simply receives more of the same kind of intelligence that is already in its possession, and thus gives greater capacity to its own individual power to think.

When the mind responds perfectly to absolute intelligence it makes conscious use of absolute intelligence in every process of thinking; and this conscious use causes the mind to steadily grow in the consciousness of absolute intelligence. The result is that the intelligence of the individual mind will constantly increase, because we invariably gain possession of those qualities of which we become conscious.

The power of absolute intelligence is unlimited, therefore, when the individual mind begins to open itself more and more to the perpetual influx of this intelligence, the mind will constantly be renewed and enlarged; the intellect will become more and more brilliant, and every action of thought will convey added power to the mind.

To give added power to the mind is to animate the mind, and to animate the mind is to invigorate the body. The youth-producing forces in the system will thereby be perpetuated because the aging process can not possibly gain a foothold so long as mind and body are growing in the power of life.

When the mind begins to consciously use absolute intelligence in every process of thinking, no effort will be required to understand what the mind may desire to understand. The light of the mind will be so clear and so strong that it can see perfectly everything that there is to be seen in its present mental world; and though the world of the growing mind is constantly being enlarged, there will be no difficulty in comprehending the larger, because so long as the mind is consciously using absolute intelligence, its entire world, however large, will always be filled with a brilliant mental light.

It is therefore evident that to keep the mind open to the full light of absolute intelligence, is to give such perfect ease and smoothness to all thinking, that hard and heavy thinking will be eliminated completely; and to remove such thinking is to remove one of the chief causes of old age.

When all thinking animates the mind and invigorates the body, both mental and physical weariness will disappear; the entire personality will ever be full of new life, which is young life. To be full of young life is to feel young, and so long as man continues to feel young he will continue to stay young.

X.

Mental States that Produce Conditions of Age, and How to Remove Them.

To perpetuate the youth of the personality, all conditions of mind and body must be normal. When these conditions are not normal the natural renewing process is interfered with, and to interfere with the renewing process is to produce the aging process.

To insure normal conditions in mind and body, every mental state must be in harmony with the principle and the purpose of life, because every mental state will produce in the system, a condition similar to itself, and every state that is not in harmony with the purpose of life will produce a condition that is adverse.

When adverse conditions enter the system, the natural processes of the system will be disturbed and misdirected, and the forces of nature will produce what the purpose of life does not aim to produce; in consequence, these forces will work against nature instead of promoting the purpose of nature.

It is natural to stay young; every natural process produces youth and perpetuates youth; therefore, every condition that is adverse to any process in nature will produce age. That which is not working with nature is working against nature.

To train the mind to produce only those mental

(96)

states that work with nature—states that will express only normal conditions in the system—the first essential is to remove adverse mental attitudes, and the second essential is to remove the three original causes of mental adversity.

These three causes are anger, fear and worry; and when combined with the four principal adverse states, will produce any and every adverse mental state that can possibly appear in the human system.

The four attitudes referred to are the heavy attitude, the serious attitude, the superficial attitude and the excited attitude.

When the mind is in a heavy or depressed attitude, the states and actions of the mind will become sluggish, and such states will produce conditions in the system that tend to ossify the cell structures.

The reason why is found in the fact that all sluggish actions in the system decrease the power of the life force, and any living thing tends to wither, dry up, harden and grow old when its life force is decreased in power.

Those mental states that are heavy also tend to depress the physical system, and the actions of depression when coming in contact with cell structures, as they invariably do, will harden and ossify those structures.

To prevent ossification is to prevent old age, because nothing can look old or feel old until it begins to ossify. Ossification, however, is not produced by the laws of nature; it comes through the violation of the laws of nature; therefore, when man no longer violates the laws of nature, there will be no ossifying process in his system, and he will continue to stay young as long as he lives.

To remove the heavy mental attitude, the mind should be trained to live constantly in the upper story of consciousness, and should place itself in touch with those superior powers in the greater nature of man that can do whatever he may wish to have done.

To dwell in mental depression is a mere habit, and is produced by the race belief that man is so limited in his powers and possibilities that he can realize only a small fraction of his normal ambition. However, when man learns the truth about himself he will know that he is not limited, but that he has the power to do what he may have the ambition to do.

When this great truth is realized, the present will become better and greater at once, and the future become as bright as the sun. There will be nothing to be depressed about; there will be nothing to worry about; there will be nothing to burden the mind with apprehensions of dangers or misfortunes yet to be, because all ills are passing away; the causes of failure and adversity are being removed by the fuller expression of that greater power from within that can do all things well, and the mind can feel its own complete emancipation.

The mind that dwells in the realization of its own greater power, knows that it can turn all things to good account, and that the closing of one door invariably causes the opening of another—another that opens the way to greater opportunities, greater attainments, greater powers and greater joys.

It is therefore evident that such a mind will never

feel depressed, but will ever live upon the mountain top of an illuminated faith, where the richness of all things can be discerned as clearly as the light of day.

The serious attitude of mind will sour the chemical elements of the system, thus producing dissolution and decay among the cells. The system will thereby be clogged with waste-matter, and what the system fails to throw off will ossify.

This is the reason why people who take all things so seriously have a hardened, wrinkled-up skin. Too much of the matter in their skin is dead matter that has withered up and turned hard. That they should look old and worn is only what could be expected under the circumstances.

To remove the serious attitude, train the mind to live in the conviction that man was made for happiness, and that the man who is filled with the greatest joy now is the greatest power for good in the world now.

The power of the smile is invincible, that is, when it comes from within. A single smile, coming from the depths of soul-joy will do more for the welfare of mankind than ten thousand sermons burdened with sadness and gloom.

The mind that learns to realize the full significance of this great truth, will completely change its attitude, and will feel serious no more.

The superficial attitude will prevent the mind from living in touch with the greater depths of life; in consequence, the mind will be unable to draw upon the greater forces of life, and will feel weak and incompetent when the limited, superficial supply of power has been exhausted.

To decrease the power of life is to cause the system to go down to weakness and age, because the lifeless cell will wither up, harden and grow old; and when the system is not in touch with the depths of greater life it will soon exhaust its life.

To live on the surface, is to use up what you have without being able to secure more; and when the original, limited supply is used up, or nearly so, the system can no longer perform its functions. The result is weakness, disease, age, and the end of personal existence.

To remove the superficial attitude, the simplest method is to daily employ the conscious mind in directing the subconscious. To place the outer mind in conscious touch with the subconscious at frequent intervals, will not only deepen and enlarge the actions of all the mental forces, but will also cause the subconscious to give expression to a larger and a larger measure of life from its own inexhaustible supply.

The excited attitude will produce confusion, discord and misdirected actions throughout the system. The energies of the system will thus be wasted, the force of life will decrease, and conditions of age will follow.

To remove this attitude the entire system should be trained to live in poise, and every thought should be so constructed that it will have an inherent tendency to produce poise.

When these four adverse attitudes are completely removed from the mind, a number of direct causes of old-age conditions will disappear, and the mind will be placed in such perfect harmony with the constructive, youth-producing forces of the system, that every effort to perpetuate youth can be promoted with the greatest of ease and efficiency.

In addition, a number of adverse mental states will cease to exist, but to eliminate all such states, the mind must emancipate itself from anger, fear and worry.

When the mind is in anger, a number of cells are destroyed, especially in the nervous system. For the creative energies to rebuild those cells at once, is practically impossible, but if they are not rebuilt at once and the waste matter removed, the system will be clogged.

However, it is only the clean body that can stay young. Waste matter, when not removed from the system will become dead matter; it will shortly harden and ossify, thus producing conditions of age.

The natural renewing process has the capacity to remove old cells—cells that have existed in the system a few weeks or a few months, and build new ones in their places, but this process does not have the capacity to replace at once new cells that anger has destroyed by the wholesale.

It is therefore evident that anger will overtax the capacity of the renewing process, in fact, completely cripple this process at times, so that its effort to keep the system in a state of youth will fail to a lesser or greater degree.

When the renewing process fails to promote its purpose, the aging process will gain a foothold in the system, and if not removed will soon cause the entire system to fall into the habit of growing old.   This habit, however, can be removed; all habits can be removed, but the prevention is always preferable to the cure.

To emancipate the mind from anger, every thought should be trained to think that all things are working together for good to him who is seeking only the good.

There will be nothing to be angry for when all things are working together for our good; we cannot be angry with those things that are for us, and all things will be for us, ever working together for our good when we seek the good, and the good only with all the power of mind and heart and soul.

When anger is completely removed, every feeling that is antagonistic will also be removed, and this is extremely important, because the antagonistic actions of mind produce resistance to all the natural forces of the system, including the forces of growth.

However, constant growth and development all through the system is absolutely necessary to the perpetuation of youth; therefore, to permit resistance, in any form, to act in the mind is to interfere with those forces that produce youth, and the perpetuation of youth will either be retarded or suppressed completely.

To continue to stay young, the mind must train itself to resist nothing, and this becomes mere simplicity when every thought is created with a desire to work in harmony with the greater life that is in everything.

When the mind is in a state of fear, the system

becomes negative, and all the constructive forces of the system will reverse their actions, thus tearing down what had previously been building. The same results will follow when the mind enters into anxious states, troubled states or states where strength is forgotten and weakness magnified.

The mental actions of grief are wasteful, and will cause decay in the tissues of the physical system. Regret, self-pity, disappointments and similar states, have the same effect, though generally in less degree.

To perpetuate youth, however, everything that is destructive or wasteful must be eliminated completely from the human system.

The selfish actions of mind will contract the cells; and all abnormal cell contractions will cause the cells to wither, dry up and ossify.

To be selfish is to be abnormally self-centered, that is, the self attempts to absolutely establish itself within itself, thus producing the contracting tendency, and every tendency that becomes a ruling force in the mind will also become a ruling force in every cell in the personality.

The selfish tendency, however, does not simply contract the cells of the body; it also contracts the faculties of the mind; and this explains why a selfish person always has a small mind, a small character, a small heart and a small soul.

The domineering actions of mind produce hard, forceful thinking, and all such thinking produces a hardening effect upon the cell structures. But the greatest enemy to perpetual youth is worry.

When the mind worries it places in action the

chief cause of stiff backs, brittle bones, dried-up tissues, ossified cells and wrinkled faces. The reason why is found in the fact that worry is the deepest of all the adverse mental states, and thereby affects the very chemical life of the system.

When the chemical forces of the system are acted upon by worry they produce false chemical elements in the cell structures, and these false elements will harden the cells the same as if they actually were calcareous deposits.

To eliminate calcareous deposits from the system has been looked upon as the secret for perpetuating youth, and many methods have been advocated; among these distilled water has been looked upon with the greatest favor, but so long as a person worries, he will not stay young, no matter how much distilled water he may drink.

When the mind worries it actually produces calcareous elements in the system just as it produces poisons when angry. Therefore, so long as a person worries his bones will become brittle, his skin will become dried up, his cells will wither, the tissues of his system will harden and ossify, his face will wrinkle, and every atom in his body will feel old and look old, regardless of how many methods, physical or metaphysical, he may employ for preserving his youth.

The elimination of worry will not alone insure the perpetuation of youth; there are also other causes of old age; but the elimination of worry is one of *the* essentials and is made possible through the constant development of a real, living faith.

The man who has real faith in the Supreme, real

faith in himself, real faith in everybody and in everything will never worry. He will know that all things are for him, because all things *are* for him who has real faith.

To have real faith in all things is to place the mind in touch with the superior life in all things, and that life is not against anything; it is *for* the advancement of everything.

Therefore, when man is in touch with that superior life—the upper region of existence, nothing is against him; all things are with him; he has nothing to worry about because all things are coming right. When all things are with us the desires of the heart will surely be granted, and we shall reach the very highest goal we may have in view.

When man enters that upper region of thought and consciousness, where he lives in touch with the universal, he actually feels that all elements, all forces, all things and all persons are with him, and to feel, even the slightest degree of worry, is impossible.

The same realization—the realization of *the truth about man's real, superior state of being*, will also eliminate fear.

To remove selfishness, the mind should cease to live for the personal self, and should live solely for the attainments and the realizations of the superior self. There is a superior something in man; this something is the real man, and to live for this something is to remove everything from human life that is not in accord with real life.

XI.

Mental States That Perpetuate Youth.

To perpetuate the youth of the personality, the states of the mind must be in harmony with the law of perpetual renewal; and in order that all mental states may be in harmony with this law, all thinking must aim to produce renewal.

To form only those states that will perpetuate youth, the mind must focus its entire attention upon the fundamental renewing process in nature, and all thinking must be made a renewing process as well as a developing process.

To promote this purpose, the first essential is to train the mind to feel young, because the body will express the same age that is felt in the mind.

Man is as he thinks in his heart, but it is only what he feels that he thinks in his heart; therefore if he mentally feels that he is growing older and older he will steadily change to look older and older; but so long as he continues to feel young he will positively continue to look young.

The average person firmly believes that he is growing old, and this belief is so deeply impressed upon his mind that he mentally feels himself growing old; every thought he thinks is therefore an age producing thought, but it is not in harmony with the living laws of nature.

(106)

Man does not feel himself growing old because nature is making him old; nature is not making him old; this feeling is his own creation, and it is thoroughly abnormal, contrary to every law in life.

The average person, having artificially produced in himself the feeling that he is growing old, will cause his personality to look older and older every year, regardless of the fact that the perpetual renewal process in nature gives him a new body every year.

To eliminate this artificial feeling of age, the mind must be trained to feel young, and only those states of mental feeling must be permitted that have a natural tendency to perpetuate youth.

To train the mind to feel young, the picture of youth should be constantly impressed upon the mind. What we repeatedly picture in mind we soon shall feel in mind, and it is what we mentally feel that determines what our mental states are to be.

To think of age is to picture upon mind conditions of age; therefore age should never be thought of or mentioned at any time, not even in the attitude of humor.

What we think of during states of humor will impress the mind just as readily as what we think of during states of serious thought; therefore, the idea of age must be eliminated completely from all thinking.

The ideas of age and the mental pictures of age that may have been previously impressed upon the mind should be removed absolutely and at once, with clear, mental pictures of youth.

When you think of yourself, think of yourself as

being young, and know that you are thinking the truth. You *are* young; the laws of nature are constantly at work perpetuating your youth, therefore, to think the truth about yourself, you must think that you are young, and think so with thought that is positive, clear and strong.

To establish this thought about yourself, the power of affirmation may be employed to the greatest advantage, but to affirm a statement of truth, it is necessary to deeply feel that the statement is the truth.

To begin the day with the statement, "I am young, because my entire being is perpetually renewed," is to place the strong, clear thought of the morning in perfect harmony with the natural process of perpetual renewal, and every state of the mind that is formed during the day will be a youth producing state.

It is well, however, to frequently repeat this statement during the day, though these repetitions should never have the slightest trace of the mechanical.

When you affirm, in thought, "I am young," make that affirmation so clear, so positive and so strong that you can feel the vibrations of youth and vigor thrill every atom in your being; and try to feel these vibrations so deeply that their actions will penetrate into the very depth of the subconscious.

To train the mind to think the truth about the renewing process that is ever keeping the body young, it is highly important to affirm the statement: "My entire being is ever young and new, because nature permits no cell to remain in my body more than a few months, when it builds a new one in its place." To this may be added, "Nature gives me a new body every year"; "My mind is new every morning," and "My life comes forth from the Creator of life every moment as fresh and as new as the flowers of the springtime."

These statements are statements of truth, and should be affirmed constantly in the whole-souled conviction that they *are* statements of truth.

To inwardly feel that these statements are true is to purify the mind from all false beliefs and from all ideas of age. The renewal process of nature will thereby be given the freedom to express the newness of the personality; there will be no adverse states of mind to cause the new body to look old, therefore the new body will always look and feel what it is; it will look young and feel young, and will ever continue to stay young.

When the mind undertakes to give deep feeling to its affirmations, a tendency towards emotionalism may be formed, but this must not be permitted.

To be moderately emotional is necessary in order to give deep feeling to thought, but this emotional feeling must not become excited, aroused or overwrought; it must be kept in perfect poise. The most powerful forces of mind are those that are deeply emotional, but that act so quietly that they appear to be perfectly still. When such forces are permeated with a strong desire to perpetuate youth, they will positively do what they desire to do.

In the use of affirmations another essential is not to confound suggestion with statements of truth. To suggest an idea to the mind without giving direct conscious thought to the fact that it is true, is a violation of mental law; and though it may prove beneficial in a superficial and temporary sense, still it is permanently detrimental to the deeper mental life.

When any idea is suggested to the mind, consciousness should be deeply impressed with the fact that this idea is true. If there is doubt as to its being the truth, it should not be suggested to the mind until the fact that it is the truth is fully realized.

The science of affirmation is to affirm only those ideas that the mind feels to be absolutely true, and then to *deeply think* of them as being true while the affirmation is being made.

The statement, "I am young," is absolutely true; it simply gives expression to a fact in nature, therefore the mind can affirm "I am young" with the full conviction that it is the truth. And the more frequently the mind makes this affirmation, in the full conviction that it is the truth, the sooner will the body begin to express what it is—perpetual youth.

The power of affirmation to produce mental states that perpetuate youth is very marked, and it is a power that should be employed daily, regardless of how many other and seemingly superior methods we may find; nevertheless the power of affirmation is insignificant in comparison with clear mental imagery.

To constantly image in mind those qualities that are distinctly the qualities of youth, is to permanently establish those mental states that perpetuate youth; and when those states are established, every action that may proceed from the mind will have youth producing power.

When every mental state is formed in the image and likeness of the state of youth the mind will actually live in a state of youth, and so long as the mind lives in such a state the personality can never grow old. The reason why is found in the fact that the conditions of the body are invariably the exact externalizations of the states of the mind.

To establish the mind in a state of mental youth, the most perfect state of youth that the imagination can picture should be constantly held before the mental vision. This picture should be looked upon, not as a mere possibility to be realized in the coming days, but as an actual reality that is at hand to be realized now.

To constantly picture the entire body as being in the life and vigor of youth will aid in producing in the mind a clear picture of absolute personal youth; but in forming this picture of personal youth no thought whatever must be given to those conditions in the body that express age, if such there should be.

To eliminate age, the mind must completely forget age, and give its whole attention to the creation of those conditions that are absolutely in a state of youth.

The imaging faculty can picture the adverse just as easily as it pictures the true, the beautiful and the ideal; and as everything that is pictured in mind will be more or less expressed in the body, no thought whatever should be given to that which is not desired.

The power of the imagination should be used exclusively in taking the mind through the many mansions of the world beautiful; but in the world beautiful old age is inconceivable. There can be no age in an ideal world, therefore there can be no thought of age in an ideal state of mind.

When the imagining faculty is properly employed it will cause the mind to *see* only the perpetual youth of the personality, because youth is real; old age is artificial, abnormal, wrong. And when the mind sees only youth in the being of man it will create only those states of mind that perpetuate youth.

The mind can think only that which it can mentally see, and the person of man is as the mind thinks; therefore, so long as the mind continues to see only those states of being that are young, the personality will continue to stay young.

To give the qualities of youth to every state of mind is the object in view, and to promote this object the mind should daily affirm the truth about the being of man—the truth that the being of man always is young through and through, and should daily give shape to those affirmations in the form of mental pictures of youth.

When the mind begins to realize the permanent reality of youth, the fact that old-age conditions are unnatural will become perfectly clear. To refuse to mould life after the likeness of the unnatural will then become second nature, and every creative force in the system will proceed to imitate the process of perpetual renewal. In consequence, every action of mind or body will tend to perpetuate youth.

The forces of the human system should imitate the fundamental forces of nature, and nature gives per-

petual youth to all things at all times. The forces of
the human system, however, invariably follow the
leading ideas of the mind, and the leading ideas are
always those ideas that are pictured upon mind with
the greatest clearness, positiveness and strength.

It is therefore evident that if the forces of the human system are to imitate the forces of nature and perpetuate the youth of the system, the imaging faculty
must constantly hold before mind the perfect picture
of youth—eternal youth.

To try to perpetuate the youth of the personality
so long as the imaging faculty pictures in mind the
idea of age is useless; and the imaging faculty will
continue to picture the idea of age so long as man
continues to believe in the reality of age. To train
the mind to give the spirit of youth to every single
idea or thought that is formed is therefore absolutely
necessary.

To train the mind in this respect, consciousness
should enter so completely into the life of the renewing
process that this process can be actually felt in the
system. This feeling should become an established
phase of consciousness, and will if given the most
prominent recognition possible at all times.

When man can actually *feel* that his entire system
is being constantly renewed all old-age beliefs and all
old-age conditions must disappear absolutely. Even
though his system be full of age—artificial age, because
there is no natural age—his body will in a year's time
change into the full vigor and appearance of youth,
after he has begun to feel the process of perpetual
renewal.

The personality may have lived for eighty years and may look as old as race thought believes such a personality should look; nevertheless, when the mind that animates that personality begins to *feel* the process of renewal and begins to *live* in the mental state of youth, the personality will begin to look young and feel young, and in less than a year will have the vigor and the appearance of one in the prime of life. And why not? Nature gives man a new body every year; this new body *is* young; then why should not this body look young and feel young?

XII.

Live For The Purpose Of Advancement, Attainment And Achievement.

To live the life of continuous advancement is to enter into the conscious possession of more and more life, and the perpetual increase of life is one of the fundamental essentials to the perpetuation of youth.

It is not possible for the aging process to gain a foothold in the human system so long as there is increase of life, because the body begins to grow old only when it begins to lose life.

The losing of life is produced by a multitude of causes; in brief, every violation of the laws of mind or body will decrease the power of human life, but the principal essential to the perpetual increase of life is to live directly for the purpose of continuous advancement.

The continuous advancement of the personality into more and more life will not only perpetuate youth, but will also prolong personal existence; the reason being that the length of personal existence depends directly upon the amount of stored-up life energy with which every cell in the personality is supplied.

To constantly recharge every cell in the human system with life energy is to cause the system to continue to live as an organized form, because it is not possible for death to take place where there is an abundance of

(115)

life; and this abundance of life will be given to the personality so long as the individual continues to advance into more and more life.

To promote continuous advancement into more and more life the first essential is to live directly for the purpose of advancement; every object in view must be larger and greater than what the present has realized, and every action that takes place in the human system must have enlargement, expansion and ascension as the ruling tendencies of its power.

To live for a definite purpose in regard to attainment and achievement is necessary; it is only through higher attainments and greater achievements that the law of continuous advancement can be promoted; therefore the desire to become much and achieve much must inspire the life of every atom in him who has resolved to perpetuate his youth.

The desire to become much and achieve much must be so strong that it is constantly felt in every fibre as an irresistible power, and it must never cease in its action. The mind must picture itself as living perpetually in a life of action, growth, attainment and achievement, and no thought whatever must be given to future retirement from active life.

The future should remain in the hands of the future; to live an active life now and to continue to live an active life now should be the one purpose to engage the whole of attention. To think of retiring from active life is to think of inactivity, and when the mind begins to think of inactivity the life of growth will be suspended.

When man ceases to grow he begins to grow old,

but he can not possibly grow old so long as he continues to grow. This growth, however, must be alive throughout the entire personality and must aim to perfect the body and develop the mind.

To promote this growth the mind should be alive with interest in all growing life, and should cooperate consciously with all growth, advancement and progress.

When this cooperation becomes a part of personal existence, the spirit of advancement can be felt in every part of the system, and when every atom *feels* advancement every atom will advance.

The advancement of every atom in the system will promote the improvement of every function, faculty and quality in personal life, providing the mind is working constructively for the attainment of every possible state of improvement, and so long as everything in body, mind and soul is being constantly improved, age will not appear.

The conditions of age are inseparably connected with inaction and retrogression; therefore, so long as the personality is absolutely full of action and progress it can not grow old; it will continue to stay young.

To promote eternal progress in the whole of man will perpetuate youth in the whole of man.

The true significance of eternal progress as applied to the individual life of man is that state of being wherein every atom, every active force, every function, every faculty, every talent, every power—in brief, wherein everything that is alive in the personality—is constantly improving upon its own life, action and purpose.

To follow the law of eternal progress everything in the human system must act for the purpose of acting better, and it is evident that nothing can deteriorate, grow old and decay that is constantly improving upon the life, the power and the efficiency of its own action.

To act for the purpose of acting better is to become better; it is to promote the very fundamental law of development, and where development is constant, age is impossible.

The development of the mind implies the expansion of consciousness, the enlargement of the intellect, the refinement of the mental qualities, and the increased efficiency of mental action. The development of the body implies the perfecting of the form, the refinement of physical sensation, the increase of the power of personal expression, the improvement of the quality of the cell-structures, the increased efficiency of functional activity, and the improvement of the personality as an instrument of the mind.

These phases of development in mind and body may all be promoted by training the life of the individual to live directly and consciously for the purpose of advancement. The various elements and forces of the human system are governed by the action of consciousness; therefore, when conscious life gives its whole life to the action of continuous advancement, everything in the human system will do the same. The entire system in general and every part of the system in particular, will advance. And to advance always is to stay young always.

To train the individual life to live for the purpose

of continuous advancement, the leading essential is to establish the conscious desire to employ all the energy of the system for the promotion of the renewing process and the growing process. It is not sufficient to simply renew the system, the system must be elevated to a more perfect state of being every time that it is renewed.

When the growing process and the renewing process are perfectly combined, the personality will continue to stay young, and will continue to express the life of youth upon higher and higher planes of being. The result will be a life that is thoroughly worth while. Such a life will continue to enrich itself from every imaginable source, and through the perpetuation of youth will have the power to enjoy those real riches in an ever-increasing measure.

The desire to employ all the energy of the system for the promotion of the growing process and the renewing process, may be established by constantly giving conscious recognition to the existence of those processes, and to the fact that man may, through the promotion of those two processes, reach any worthy goal that he may have in view.

The mind is so constituted that it will naturally develop the desire to do that which is constantly recognized as the real secret to its goal in view; and when this real secret is known to be the law upon which the very purpose of life is based, the desire in question will develop into far greater strength in much less time.

To promote continuous advancement is the purpose of life; therefore, to constantly recognize this purpose as the secret to every worthy goal in view, is to place the mind in harmony with those laws in life that have the power to reach any worthy goal in view; and when the mind is placed in touch with the power that can, it immediately gains the desire to do what this power can do.

It is therefore evident that when the mind is placed in perfect touch with the law of advancement, the law upon which the entire universe is based, a desire to do what this law aims to do will develop, and the ruling desire of the mind will be to advance, to advance eternally, and in every way imaginable.

To employ all the energies of the system for the promotion of advancement will thus become second nature; the individual will live to live more, and will desire to live more in order that higher attainments and greater achievements may be realized.

When the mind gains this desire there will be no satisfaction in the mere gain of that which has previously been held in view; satisfaction does not come to such a mind through the gain of things, but through the continuous advancement of life towards greater and greater things; such a mind gains "the greatest joy of all joys—the joy of going on."

To be satisfied with the present is to cause inactivity in one or all of the phases of mind, and when action and growth are on the wane, age invariably begins.

To perpetuate youth, the mind must find its satisfaction, its contentment and its joy in nothing less than continuous advancement towards the larger, the greater and the superior. The mind must be trained, to be satisfied only when it is moving forward; and every mind that is placed in harmony with the fundamental purpose of life will never cease to move forward.

To gain the greatest good and the greatest joy from that which we have possession of now, it is necessary to advance now. The mind that is inactive enjoys nothing, appropriates nothing, even though it may be surrounded by the greatest riches that the world can produce. It is the growing mind that appropriates the richness of life, and the mind gains enjoyment only from that which it has appropriated.

The growing mind is the advancing mind; therefore to be contented and happy now it is necessary to advance now; and to continue to advance is to continue to stay young.

XIII.

Love Your Work, and Know That You Can Work as Long as You Can Love.

To supply the system with an abundance of life is one of the great essentials in the perpetuation of youth; and there is nothing that awakens more life than the act of giving love to everything that one may do. Love also awakens the finer elements of life, those elements that invariably give newness, freshness, soundness, briskness, sprightliness, vigor and youth to the personality.

To work is to give expression to energy, and to love that work is to give animation to the energy that is being expressed. When this energy is animated, that is, given soul, it is not mechanical, and to prevent physical or mental energy from being mechanical is highly important.

When the energy that is given action in the system has a mechanical action, it soon wears itself out and wearies the system; but when this energy is animated it multiplies its own power while in action, and thereby increases the life, the power and the vigor of the system.

To weary the system is to decrease the normal life of the system, and if this decrease is frequently repeated the normal supply of life will not be sufficient to maintain the action of the natural functions; nor will the renewing process have sufficient power to fully promote its work. The result will be the beginning of age because the aging process always begins when the life force is on the wane.

Those who desire to stay young must never permit themselves to become tired; and they will never feel tired if they never think of being tired, never speak of being tired and never fail to love their work.

It is not natural to become tired; it is an abnormal condition produced by the mechanical action of the energies of the system. This mechanical action, however, is completely eliminated by the presence of a strong love for the work in which the person may be engaged.

The reason why the average person never gets tired from play but always gets tired from work, is because he loves the former but does not love the latter. The work is mechanical, the play is not; therefore the one wearies while the other exhilarates. The work, however, would never be mechanical if it were loved, and it is possible to love work just as much as we love play.

The mechanical action of the system—the grinding action—also has a tendency to take life force out of the cells, and when the cells are deprived of this life force they begin to dry up, to wither, to become hard and ossify. But ossification must be prevented if youth is to be retained; therefore everything that produces ossification must be completely eliminated from the system.

To work in a dull, indifferent, mechanical, lifeless, automatic attitude is to produce conditions in the system that will ossify the cells and thus bring age upon yourself. No person, therefore, can afford to work in such attitudes, nevertheless, it is in these attitudes that the great majority perform their work; and that the aging process should be in action everywhere is only what is to be expected under the circumstances.

To force oneself to do what one thinks is his duty to do, will also produce the same hard, mechanical actions, and such actions invariably grind the life force out of the cells, thereby causing the cells to dry up, ossify and grow old.

The remedy is to love everything that one may do; and when one loves his work he will not have to force himself to do what he has to do; he will want to do it. He will thereby receive the necessary power to do his work with ease, because that which is animated with love is always given additional life and power.

The man who loves his work will gain the power to work as long as he can love, because to love work is to constantly increase the capacity for work. Such a man will never be superannuated, nor placed upon the retired list; he will be so valuable that the world will not permit him to retire, nor will he have any desire to retire. To him who loves his work, work is a pleasure and is one of the great additions to life.

The present demand for young men everywhere in the industrial world has nothing to do with years; it is the men with brains, vigor and life that are wanted; how long they have lived upon earth is of no consequence. The majority of those who have passed the half century mark, however, have permitted their brain-cells to ossify; they are therefore no longer competent, and younger men are in demand; but any man who will eliminate ossification from his system will become more brilliant, more powerful and more useful the longer he lives, and the industrial world will continue indefinitely to want his service, even at his own price.

Learn to stay young and the opportunities of the future will be many times as great as those of the present. The longer you live the more you will know, and so long as the system continues in youth and vigor, added knowledge and experience means added capacity and power.

To him who has learned to stay young, the coming of more years means the coming of more intelligence, more talent, more power, more capacity, more usefulness, more real life, more real joy and more of everything that is rich and beautiful in the world. He does not dread the coming of more years, because to him it does not mean weakness, age and empty idleness; instead, it means youth combined with experience, vigor combined with opportunity, visions of attainments combined with real attainments, desire combined with realization, the love of the rich and the beautiful combined with the possession of the rich and the beautiful, and the capacity to enjoy combined with the possession of that which can give joy.

The work of the average person seems hard, and the reason is found in the fact that the action he employs at his work uses up energy instead of developing the power of energy. The action of work should have the tendency to arouse more and more of the energy that is latent in the system, and it is evident that when

work has this tendency the work itself will increase
the power of the system instead of decreasing that
power as it usually does.

To give work the tendency to call forth the latent
energy of the system, the secret is to love that work.
The action of love will deepen the action of work, thus
placing the action of work in touch with the depths
of inexhaustible life. The action of love will also
give a constructive tendency to the action of work.
The power of love is always constructive and tends
to give to everything with which it may come in
contact, a desire to build, expand, enlarge, develop,
increase.

The fundamental purpose of work is to build
things, but the action of work can also be caused to
build the builder; in fact, when the action of work is
wholly constructive it will build the builder while the
builder is building things, and the action of work will
invariably become constructive when the builder loves
his work.

It is therefore evident that when a person loves
his work that work will become a power of development, and instead of being a cause of wear and tear
in the human system it becomes a cause of greater
power, greater capacity and greater ability.

When the individual works scientifically his work
will make him stronger, more able and more competent. And to work scientifically the first principle is
to love the work with all the power of heart and soul;
the second principle is to *think* that all work will
build, develop and strengthen the worker. To enter
into all work, thinking that it will act in the capacity

of a developing power, is to mentally direct all the energies of the system to build up the system while on their way to be used in the building of things. The energies of the system will do whatever they are directed to do, and we unconsciously direct them to develop our minds and bodies when we love our work and work in the conviction that those energies are wholly constructive in all their normal action.

When an energy is constructive it will necessarily have a constructive effect upon the system wherein it is generated and upon the person by whom it is employed; that is, the person who works with that energy will be constantly developed by the constructive tendency of that energy. And all energy that is employed in the action of work becomes constructive when the worker thoroughly loves his work and lives in the constructive mental attitude.

The person who loves his work will also do his work better, and the reason is that love gives greater building power to all energy. When we love what we are doing we are at our best and will naturally do our best; we call forth the finest elements of life, the finest creative forces and the finest forces of thought; in consequence, the work done will be the best that can be produced in our present state of development.

To thoroughly love the work in hand will therefore become a means to personal advancement, and as the love of the work in hand will also perpetuate youth, we secure from the same cause both youth and advancement—a most happy combination, indeed.

The path to great attainments and great achievements is open only to those who have learned to love their work, and for those who have acquired this art the future has many riches in store; in fact, whenever a person learns to thoroughly love his work, he finds the secret to continuous advancement and perpetual increase; and in addition he will inherit eternal youth.

The fact that the love of the work in hand will completely eliminate the mechanical element from that work, is one of the most important of all facts in human life, because so long as work is mechanical it will be inferior work. Mechanical work will also grind the life force out of the cells, thus causing the cells to wither, dry up, harden, ossify and grow old. Neither youth nor advancement are therefore possible so long as work is mechanical, and all work, whether physical or mental, that we do not love, is mechanical.

The action of every force in the system becomes a mechanical action if that action is not animated by a strong love for the doing of that which called forth the action. To completely eliminate the mechanical from every action in the system we must learn to love everything that we do, or resolve to do only that which we can love with all the power of heart and soul.

To learn to love our work the first essential is to choose that work that we think will prove most congenial; though if such work is not to be had at present, we must remember that we can learn to love anything that we may be called upon to do, and whatever we are called upon to do, before we begin, we should affirm with all the power of heart and soul, "I will love to do it."

To constantly affirm "I love my work" will steadily develop a strong love for that work, providing the statement is made in the depth of subconscious feeling. No affirmation, however, will have any effect upon the system in any way unless it is impressed upon the subconscious, and the same is true of thinking in general.

To think of your work as something that you dearly love is necessary, and if that love becomes a strong passion the gain will be far greater. No person should ever think or say that he does not love his work; to do so is to go down to failure and old age. When we have work to do that does not seem congenial at first, we should make it congenial for the time being by giving it love—strong love, and in the greatest possible abundance. This is not mere sentiment; it is exact scientific thinking, and he who applies it will find that it pays.

To thoroughly love what we are doing now is to enter the path to something that we will love better. He who makes himself as congenial as possible to everything will soon develop such a strong congenial power that he will attract everything that is congenial. By dealing with all things as if they were his own, he will find those things that actually are his own. In other words, the man who loves his work with all the power of his love will develop such a large love for work that he will naturally attract work that is as large as himself.

To find work that corresponds with our capacity, and that is exactly to our liking, the above is the secret. He who always loves his work will always have work that he loves. He will also advance constantly, and in addition will inherit eternal youth.

XIV.

Perpetual Enjoyment Goes Hand In Hand With Perpetual Youth.

The happy mind alone is normal, and to stay young the mind must be normal, it must be in perfect harmony with nature.

To be happy the mind must have enjoyment; the mind is happy only when something is being enjoyed, be that something tangible or intangible; therefore, if the mind is to continue to be normal and continue to stay young, enjoyment must be continuous.

To secure perpetual youth it is first necessary to secure perpetual enjoyment, that is, every moment of life must be enjoyed, and enjoyment must be gained from everything that enters into life.

To enjoy every moment of life the mind must be trained to enjoy the living of life, and it will be found that when consciousness gains a perfect realization of life itself, simply *to be* is joy everlasting.

To depend upon things, events or circumstances for happiness, is to find but the shadow; real joy comes only when things, events and circumstances are animated with the living of real life—the soul of tangible existence.

It is the soul of things that gives joy, and it can give joy without being tangibly expressed through things, but the greatest joy comes invariably from the largest expression of soul through the most wholesome condition of things.

To seek an abundance of wholesome enjoyment in the world of things is therefore necessary to give richness, fullness and completeness to the expression of that perpetual joy that comes from the living of soul.

To be happy every single moment, must be one of the chief aims of every mind, but happiness should not be sought for the mere purpose of gratifying the desires of the person. Happiness should be sought for its own sake, and for the greater richness of life that is always realized through continued attitudes of joy.

The period of enjoyment should be extended indefinitely, and should not be confined to the earlier periods of personal existence. To be true to himself, every person must be happy as long as he lives, but if he is not happy as long as he lives he is not true to himself.

The world of false belief declares, "Let the young enjoy themselves while they can; they will get old soon enough." Also, "We are young but once, let us enjoy ourselves while we are young; when age comes there is neither desire nor capacity for enjoyment any more." The language of darkness and despair; the language of those who have placed themselves in bondage to false race-thought, and do not know that they are others than free men thinking their own original thought.

The belief that the young must enjoy themselves while they can, causes the majority of those who are

still young to cram several times as much "enjoyment" into the space of a few years as the consciousness of those years can possibly appropriate.
The result is that the greater part of the enjoyment
that is sought fails to give joy, but instead wearies
the mind and hurries the day of the "settled life."

When the "settled life" begins, the aging process
takes a firm foothold in the system, and will soon demonstrate the power of its presence.

When children are taught that they can stay young
as long as they may live, and that they may enjoy
themselves as long as they continue to stay young,
they will not cram a few short years of youth with
every pleasure that may present itself; they will know
that there is time to enjoy everything, to enjoy everything right, and to seek the most wholesome enjoyment of everything.

When children are taught these great facts they
will not only seek enjoyments of quality, but they will
also seek to develop greater capacity for enjoyment.
The development of greater capacity to enjoy will
prove profitable in the light of the fact that enjoyment
may continue all through life, and that personal existence may be enjoyed in greater and greater measure.

The belief that we are young but once is true,
but that "once" continues as long as we live a normal
life; we grow old only through the violation of natural law, but nature has the power to restore youth
to any personality that returns to the life that is normal in the full sense of that term.

To live in the belief that youth is for a short period

only is to expect age, and to expect age is to produce age.

To live in the belief that we can enjoy ourselves only when we are "young" is not only to overdo the life of mere pleasure, but pleasure will be sought for the mere gratification of the mind of sense, and pleasures that simply gratify the superficial life are weakening. Besides, such pleasures never have quality, and to seek pleasures of quality is of the highest importance.

We invariably grow into the likeness of that which we enjoy; therefore, to enjoy the superficial, the sensuous and the materialistic is to become materialistic and ordinary; it is to waste the limited energies of the personal life without giving any attention to the appropriation of the limitless energies from the great within.

To promote the perpetuation of youth the race-belief about pleasure must be entirely reversed, because pleasure is an inseparable part of life, but that part is not properly played by those who accept the race-belief on the subject. The race believes that pleasure is incidental and that happiness is something, the cause of which no man knows; therefore, it comes and goes regardless of what man may think or do. This, however, is not the truth; happiness can be produced by man at will, and to be true to himself he must give happiness to every moment of his personal existence.

To seek enjoyment is just as important as to seek wisdom or virtue, and wholesome pleasures are just as valuable in the moral world as righteous thoughts.

When happiness is absent man has gone astray and when pleasure is sought no more, man has lost his mental grip on the meaning and purpose of life.

The mind that is alive needs pleasure just as much as the body that is alive needs nourishment, and to perpetuate the youth of the personality both mind and body must be thoroughly alive. When the mind is deprived of pleasure it ceases to live the life of youth, it begins to grow old, and an old mind will soon cause the body to look as old as the mind feels. To give the mind enjoyment—perpetual enjoyment—is therefore necessary if the youth of the personality is to be retained.

To provide the mind with perpetual enjoyment is a problem that is easily solved when the fact is recognized that life itself is made for happiness, and that the happy mind alone is normal. When the mind is normal, happiness is a natural consequence; therefore to be happy at all times, all that is necessary is to keep the mind normal at all times.

The normal mind is the mind that is in harmony with the laws of nature, and as the principal laws of nature in the life of man are the laws of growth and renewal, the mind that aims to perpetually renew itself and to promote its own perpetual development, will readily assume the normal mental state.

The normal state, however, can be perfected into higher and higher degrees of realization, and to promote this perfecting process for the purpose of increasing the capacity for enjoyment, the mind should be trained to appreciate the joy of life on all the planes of existence—the physical, the mental and the spiritual.

The reason why happiness in the life of the average person is not constant is found in the fact that enjoyment is sought on one or two planes only, instead of in all three. To give the mind perpetual enjoyment each plane must exercise its power to produce happiness, and the more frequently during each day that these three powers are brought into expression the greater will be the joy secured.

To seek pleasure only through the body is to secure only the cheapest kind of pleasure; to seek pleasure only through the mind is to find a degree of intellectual satisfaction but no real happiness; to seek pleasure only through the soul is to find those joys that secret moments alone can receive; they do not touch the personal life of every day unless the life of every day is made to touch the soul.

When the conscious ego undertakes to make body, mind and soul the one complete source of all pleasure, the pleasures of the body will be refined and will, in consequence, produce far greater happiness; the pleasures of the mind will be given warmth from the body and ecstasy from the soul, and will thereby become a continual feast of sublime richness; the pleasures of the soul will be given full expression through mind and body, and will therefore give continual joy to every moment of personal existence.

The mind should be taught at the earliest possible moment to seek enjoyment from all the three planes of life, and should be taught to combine these three into the most perfect unity of thought imaginable. The result will be perpetual enjoyment, harmony of expression and perfect personal equilibrium.

To combine the three sources of pleasure into one, the first essential is to recognize the fact that happiness is a continuous force in the human system, and that the expression of that force would be continuous if consciousness was always free to receive and transmit that expression. But consciousness is not always free, because the only free consciousness is that consciousness that is conscious of the whole of life—body, mind and soul—all three at all times.

When the conscious ego seeks to draw pleasure from the body alone, consciousness is confined in the physical, and a confined consciousness is not a free consciousness. The same is true when the conscious ego seeks pleasure from the mind only or the soul only. To be free, consciousness must not be confined in any one plane, but must be permitted to encompass all planes. When in that state consciousness is in touch with the force of happiness from *every* source, and in consequence the individual will always be conscious of happiness—will always feel the real, sublime, immeasurable joy of life.

To live is to create happiness; the living of life gives joy to life, therefore so long as life continues there is a continuous force of happiness in the human system, and this force can be felt at all times when consciousness is free to feel what is in action in the whole of real life. And this freedom of consciousness is secured when consciousness is conscious of body, mind and soul—all three at all times.

The freedom of consciousness to feel the force of happiness from every source at all times will cause the mind to be nourished with that something that is indispensable to the perpetual aliveness of mind. The mind that is constantly full of joy is always alive, and the mind that is always alive will always stay young.

When the mind gains enjoyment from only one of the three sources it will soon weary of the joy, the reason being that the joy is incomplete, it does not give aliveness to the whole system; but the mind will never weary of joy when it seeks enjoyment from all three sources of joy—body, mind and soul, because such a joy will produce perpetual aliveness throughout the entire being of man, and that which is alive in every part can not be weary in any part.

To perpetuate the youth of the personality, every part of the human system must be thoroughly alive at all times; to lose life is to grow old and die, and this perpetual aliveness will always continue so long as the mind is supplied with real joy from the three great sources of joy. Therefore, perpetual enjoyment and perpetual youth are one and inseparable.

XV.

Live In The Upper Story, And On The Sunny Side.

When we live in the upper story we always look younger, and we always look older when we live in the lower story. In like manner we look older when we live on the shady side and younger when we live on the sunny side. These are facts that have been universally demonstrated, and are therefore highly important to those who have resolved to stay young.

The reason why the appearance of the personality, as to age, is affected by these different attitudes of mind may be readily found through a careful study of the chemistry of life. Conditions of age or conditions of youth are chemical conditions, and chemical conditions in the human system may be directly modified by changing attitudes of mind.

To live in the upper story of mind is to gain consciousness of more life, and the increase of life invariably produces rejuvenation. This same attitude also produces an expanding condition in the mind; the mind feels larger when we live in the upper story, and what we feel in the mind will be expressed in the body. In consequence the expanding actions of mind will affect the chemical actions of the body and will cause the cells to expand to their full capacity. Expanded cells look young and are full of vigor, while withered cells look old and are almost lifeless. To

(138)

give the cells of the body the expanding tendency will also cause those cells to constantly grow and develop; and where all the cells of the body are growing cells, old-age conditions can not possibly gain a foothold.

Where the mind lives in the lower story, all the actions of mind become depressed and contracted, and according to the same law the cells of the body will contract, wither, feel weak and look old. Such cells will soon begin to ossify, and when ossification sets in the entire system will begin to grow old. Mental depression also has a tendency to check the forces of growth, and the human system always begins to grow old when it ceases to grow.

To live on the dark side of life is to place the mind in a pessimistic attitude, and while in this attitude the mind sees only failure, defeat, the smallness of things and the uselessness of things. Such thoughts and mental states produce retrograding tendencies, and when such tendencies begin to act in the body, the forces of growth will be reversed. The cells of the body will consequently go down to weakness, decay, age and death. Nothing can grow and develop where darkness prevails, and perpetual growth in every part of the system is necessary if youth is to be retained

To live on the sunny side of life is to place the mind in the attitude of progress and advancement. It is the law that the mind invariably moves toward that something upon which its attention is directed; therefore, when the mind is facing the sunny states of life it will create within itself a tendency to move towards the light, and to move towards the light is to enter constantly into more and more light. To increase the light of the mind is to promote the advancement of the entire being of man, and continuous advancement invariably means perpetual youth. To live in mental brightness will also polish, refine and spiritualize the entire system, and while the refining or spiritualizing process is in action, retrogression, ossification, decay and age are impossible.

When the mind is living on the sunny side, every action of the mind becomes constructive, everything in the system is purified as it is in the power of sunshine to produce purity everywhere, whether the sunshine be physical or mental; and all the elements and conditions of the personality are made wholesome. It is the tendency of cheerfulness, brightness and mental sunshine to make everything in the system pure and wholesome, and when the mind is in continual sunshine, only that which is wholesome will exist in the human system. Conditions of age, however, are not wholesome, therefore they can not exist in a system where everything is wholesome, that is, when man is living on the sunny side.

To train the mind to live on the sunny side the greater possibilities that are latent in all life should be constantly analyzed with the deepest of interest. The mind that knows what is possible in the vast domains of the greater human mentality, will never become pessimistic nor depressed. To such a mind life is exceedingly rich, and every moment is not only a promise of greater things but a positive assurance of realizations that far transcend the life of the present. There is nothing but brightness in store for the mind that sees the richest possibilities of life, and that is constantly moving forward into the fuller realization of those riches. The greater good and the greater joy must inevitably develop in such a life.

To hold the greater possibilities of life constantly before the mind is necessary, because the mental eye should be kept single upon all that is rich and promising. When the mind is trained to see only that which has sunshine in it—that which looks bright and promising, it will continue to live in brightness, and to live in brightness is to realize every promise that brightness has in store.

When there seems to be no sunshine in the external world, the mind should turn its attention wholly upon the sunshine that always does exist in the internal world. To look into the deeper life is to find unlimited possibilities ready for man to develop, and to see these riches of real life will give sunshine and joy to any mind. To know what man can attain and accomplish is to give perpetual sunshine to the mind, and this any mind may know by turning attention upon the greatness of the great within. To live in the larger world and to move constantly forward into the fuller realization of the larger world, is to live in the light of the greater life, and to live in this light is to be *in* real sunshine—the sunshine that makes existence an endless moment of everlasting joy.

To train the mind to live in the upper story of thought and consciousness the first essential is to give clear recognition to the fact that there is an upper region of mental life; and the second essential is to give attention only to those thoughts, ideas, feelings and states of mind that have an ascending tendency. To live in a worried, depressed mental atmosphere and to enter into close sympathy with such mental conditions is to give mind a descending tendency. In consequence, the mind will enter the lower story of consciousness, where everything is clouded, confused and listless. While the mind is in this attitude all work is hard work, and no faculty or mental force is at its best. But when the mind is in the upper story, everything that is done is done well and without the least effort.

When the mind is in the upper story it has more life and power, and intelligence is far more brilliant; the reason why is found in the fact that all the ascending forces of mind are creative, that is, they generate what may be termed a form of mental electricity—a force that produces both power and light. And to live in the upper story is to cause every action of the mind to become an ascending or rising action. To live in the lower story, however, is to cause every action of mind to go down, and to go down is to enter weakness, darkness and nothingness. That it is impossible to do anything of real worth while living in the lower story is therefore evident.

To train the mind to live in the upper story, it is necessary to "count everything joy"; the happy actions of mind are invariably rising actions, while those actions that are not animated with joy will move in the opposite direction, thus taking the mind down to the lower story. To count everything joy becomes a matter of ease when the meaning, the purpose and the possibilities of life are understood, because to know life is to live for the purpose of living a greater life, and in the life of him who lives for a greater life all things will work together for the building of the greater life.

The fact that all things work together for good to him who desires only the good, and who desires the good with all the power of heart and soul, is a fact that has been universally demonstrated; therefore the mind that desires only the good can readily count everything joy. To such a mind everything will produce joy, and the more fully he enters into the soul of his expectation of joy from everything, the more joy he will receive from everything. It is also a demonstrated fact that he who counts everything joy will, through that attitude of mind, cause everything to produce joy.

That with which we come in contact in life invariably responds to the actions of our mental attitudes. Man is the master of his environments, his conditions and his circumstances, but he masters these things, not by trying to control them, but by controlling himself, by placing himself in those mental attitudes through which the forces of his own being will be directed, to produce what he desires to produce. And the way the forces of his own being are moving, the forces of his environment will move also. This is one of the great immutable laws of life, and whoever will apply this law in his every action will place his own life absolutely in his own hands.

When the individual mind counts everything joy, and lives in the happy thought that all things work together for good, the forces of that mind are directed to work only for the good, and for the producing of

joy in everything that transpires. In consequence, all
the forces of environment will also work together for
the good of that individual and will cause everything
in the world of circumstance to give joy to that individual. Every action in such a life will be an ascending action, and the mind will constantly live in the
upper story.

To train the mind to live in the upper story it is
also necessary to live in the happy thought that all
things can be turned to good account; and it is the
truth that you are turning all things to good account
when you *feel* that you are turning everything in yourself to good account. The forces of your own environment will invariably turn the way you turn; it is therefore extremely important that everything in your own
being be turned towards the greater goal in view. It
is necessary, however, that the actions of your turning be strong and positive. What you decide to do
you must do with all the power of mind and soul, and
what you desire you must desire with a force that is
absolutely irresistible. But this force must not be
domineering; the domineering force is the weakest
force of all; the strong force is deep and irresistible,
but so calm, so gentle and so silent that it conquers
without apparently making the slightest effort to do
so.

To turn all things to good account, and to continue to turn all things to better and better account, is
to perpetually enlarge the individual life, and to perpetually elevate the sphere of action of that life. In
consequence, the upper region of mind will be the
principal dwelling place, and this region will invariably

face the sunshine of superior existence. Every action of the mind will move upward and onward, and will thereby not only promote advancement, but will also tend to keep the whole of life in the upper world. To live in the upper world of thought is to live in perpetual joy and perpetual sunshine, and according to laws previously mentioned, perpetual youth will be the natural result.

To cause the mind to live perpetually in the upper story and on the sunny side, it is necessary to eliminate dependence upon things, that is, the position of things must not determine the position of the mind, nor must the action of circumstances determine what the mind is to think and feel. Things were made to depend upon the mind, and when the mind depends upon itself, things will arrange themselves to suit the needs and desires of the mind. When the mind determines its own position and attitude regardless of the position of things, things will change their position in accord with the purpose of the mind.

When the mind determines what it is to think and feel regardless of what circumstances may suggest, circumstances will change and will begin to act in accord with that thought and that feeling that the mind has decided to pursue. When the mind ceases to be moved by things, things will place themselves at the disposal of the mind, and may be moved by the mind in any manner desired. In consequence, the mind may continue without any effort whatever to live in any attitude that may be necessary to promote its purpose in view, whether present circumstances favor that attitude or not; but circumstances will soon begin to favor that attitude, and begin to aid the mind in promoting its purpose, if the mind continues in its own favored attitude absolutely unmoved and undisturbed.

To gain this supreme control over its own position will enable the mind to remain constantly in the upper story and on the sunny side, regardless of the fact that many things in the outer world may tend to draw thought and consciousness down into darkness and depression, and by remaining undisturbed in the upper story, and on the sunny side, the mind will cause the forces of adverse circumstances to change, and become friendly the very moment they come in contact with the power of its ascending action.

It is therefore evident that the mind can be so thoroughly trained to live in the upper story and on the sunny side that those attitudes will become second nature. In consequence, many causes of old-age conditions will be removed and several of the principal causes of perpetual youth will be promoted to the highest degree. Among these we find growth, progress, advancement and development, and the mind should live firmly in the conviction that old age can not possibly enter the human system so long as the forces of growth and development are in full, continuous action.

XVI.

The Ideal, the Beautiful, the Worthy and the Great Should Be the Constant Companions of the Soul.

When the ideal, the great, the worthy and the beautiful are chosen as constant companions, the soul invariably enters a transcending mental atmosphere, and such an atmosphere is indispensable to the perpetuation of youth. The reason being that the mental atmosphere in which the soul lives, determines, to a very great extent, the nature of those conditions that appear in the personality. The transcending atmosphere tends to elevate, expand and develop the mind, thus promoting growth which is inseparable from youth, while mental atmospheres that are not transcending tend to produce the opposite effect, and all the conditions of age will inevitably follow.

The mind that lives in the ideal forgets age, because in the consciousness of the ideal everything partakes of the newness of youth; everything is in a state of youth, being formed in the likeness of that which ever is absolute, and in the absolute the conditions of age can not possibly exist. The conditions of age are conditions of imperfection, incompleteness and unnaturalness; such conditions therefore can not exist in the ideal, and to live in the ideal is to eliminate age from consciousness.

To eliminate all thought of age completely from consciousness, that is, to absolutely forget age, is one of the principal essentials to the perpetuation of youth, because when the mind absolutely forgets age it will naturally think of youth and youth only. To constantly think of youth is to constantly impress upon the subconscious the idea of youth; this will cause the subconscious mind to develop and express the conditions of youth; in consequence, the entire personality will feel young, and we always look as young as we feel.

When the mind lives in the ideal and is constantly in touch with that which has quality, superiority and worth, all the elements of mind will tend to give expression to the best that they may contain, and this is another essential to the perpetuation of youth. To continue to stay young it is necessary to promote the perpetual growth of all the qualities of the personality, but it is not possible to promote growth unless everything that is involved in the process of growth, continues to give expression to its very best.

The process of growth is a rising above the conditions of the present; it is the transforming of the largest and the best into something that is larger and better; and to transform and develop the best and give act upon the best; we must be in our

To perpetu: expression to our very best.
pass through ate youth, the entire personality must
to promote thi continuous process of development;
sonality must s development, every part of the per-
always be at its best; but nothing

can be at its best unless it continues to live in the ideal, and selects for its mental companions, those things that have high quality and worth. It is therefore evident that if the body is to stay young the soul must live in that ideal state where everything always is young; where everything continues to act in such high states of being that conditions of incompleteness are constantly being transcended; and as age is a condition of incompleteness, it can not possibly exist in such a life.

To live in the transcending atmosphere is to place the mind above the forces of environment, above the influence of the external world; the actions of mind will therefore not be determined by external circumstances but by the superior aims of the inner mentality. And this is extremely important in the perpetuation of youth, because the mind that has resolved to stay young must not permit itself to be influenced by the appearance of age, but must cause all its actions to be governed by the power of its own determination to stay young.

When the actions of the mind are being governed or modified by external circumstances, the states of the mind will be created, more or less, in the likeness of those circumstances; in consequence, the mind will not grow into the likeness of its own ideals, and will therefore fail to realize the objects in view. To prevent the conditions of external circumstances from impressing themselves upon the mind, the mind must place itself in the closest touch possible with the ideal, the great, the worthy and the beautiful. When the mental eye is single upon the ideal, it will not be impressed by anything that is not ideal.

The mind is impressed only by those things that may enter its atmosphere; therefore, if the mind is to avoid completely those impressions that are not wanted, it must surround itself with an ideal atmosphere—an atmosphere that excludes inferiority in the same manner as light excludes darkness. To produce such an atmosphere the mind must dwell with superiority, because the thoughts of the mind are similar to those things that the mind chooses as its companions, and the atmosphere of the mind is composed of its own thoughts.

The mind has the power to create its own atmosphere, to surround itself with a mental world that corresponds exactly to its own ideals, and it exercises this power by choosing its own subjects of thought; in turn, however, the mind grows into the likeness of its own atmosphere; therefore, to promote the perpetuation of youth the mind must live in a mental atmosphere that is animated with a strong growing tendency—a tendency that works ceaselessly for the enlargement, the development and the spiritualization of the entire being of man.

When the mind lives constantly with the elements of greatness, everything in the being of man will awaken its own capacity to produce greatness. The faculties of the mind will expand and develop, and the cells of the body will be aroused from their semi-alive condition and be thoroughly charged with life and power. These cells will be transformed from their withered up condition and will begin to give expression to the fullness of their own inherent capacity. In consequence, the entire personality will eliminate the conditions of old age, because such conditions can exist only in cells that are withered, dried up, ossified or depressed.

To place the mind in touch with the power of greatness is to awaken every atom in the human system to new life and new endeavor; every part of the system will proceed to out-do itself, to transcend itself and to outgrow completely its own limited conditions. The entire system will thereby pass through an absolute transformation; the old will pass away, and all things will become new. When the entire system is constantly passing through such a process, every part of the system will constantly renew itself, and the entire system will constantly pass through such a process if the mind continues to live in perfect touch with the power of greatness.

There can be no condition of age while the human system is constantly being renewed, expanded and enlarged; therefore, the man that is constantly growing in greatness will never grow old. To enter the greater is to enter the new; to enter the new is to give expression to the new, and to continue to give expression to the new is to continue to stay young.

To live in the world of the beautiful is to impress the mind more and more with the idea of the beautiful; this idea will awaken in the human system the power that can beautify the human system, because every idea that gains a foothold in mind will tend to awaken those powers that are similar to itself. To awaken the beautifying power is to cause all the elements, qualities and expressions of the human system to become more beautiful, and everything becomes younger, looks younger and feels younger when it becomes more beautiful. To make the body look beautiful is to make the body look young, and the reason why is found in the fact that the chemical actions of the interior beautifying process tend to produce conditions of youth.

The beautifying process, however, must proceed from the subconscious, and to cause this process to become established in the subconscious the soul should live constantly in the highest realms of the world beautiful.

To think beautiful thoughts is to awaken that power within us that can develop the beautiful in our own minds and bodies, providing those thoughts have *soul*, and the same power that develops the beautiful will also produce the conditions of youth. To place in action any beautifying process that comes trom within is to perpetuate the youth of the personality, and that personality that is ever becoming more beautiful in life, feeling, form and expression, will never grow old. But it is not sufficient to simply preserve that beauty that nature has originally given; to perpetuate the qualities of youth, the qualities of beauty must ever be made more and more beautiful, and this becomes possible when the soul ascends perpetually into higher and higher states of the beautiful.

When the soul grows in the consciousness of the beautiful, higher and higher degrees of the beautifying power of life will be placed in expression, and as the personality always grows into the likeness of these expressions from within, the personality will become more and more beautiful; in consequence, the qualities of youth will be retained. It is not possible, however, for the soul to grow in the consciousness of the beautiful unless the life of the individual is made beautiful, and every thought created in the likeness of that state of the beautiful that we think of as our highest ideal.

XVII.

To Love Always is to be Young Always.

To perpetuate the youth of the personality, a full expression of life is necessary, and to promote this expression the power of love must be constant and strong. To stay young it is necessary to *live,* and to live it is necessary to live more.

When the power of life ceases to increase it will begin to decrease, and the decrease of life is one of the chief causes of old age. To prevent this decrease, however, it is only necessary to love always, to permeate the entire human system with the interior actions of a perfect love.

The action of the love-principle not only perpetuates the increase of life, but it also tends to bring forth into expression the newness of real life. The reason for this is found in the fact that the actions of love will arouse more creative energy, both in the body and in the mind, than any other action; and to increase the power of creative energy is to promote re-creation.

Those creative energies that are awakened by the power of love always tend to create the ideal, because the tendency of love is toward the ideal; therefore when the power of love is strong in the human system, there will be a strong tendency to reproduce the entire system in the likeness of the

(154)

ideal. To change into the likeness of the ideal is to change from the old to the new; in consequence, the elements of youth will perpetuate their existence.

To dwell in the life of a true marriage will aid remarkably in the perpetuation of youth, not because the action of sex has any power to perpetuate youth, but because a true marriage tends to increase the expression of a higher and a higher quality of love. The expression of love, however, will not by itself, perpetuate the youth of the personality; the other principles of scientific thought and action must also be applied, but a strong, high, ever-growing love-nature is one of the fundamental essentials.

Those who have not a companion with whom to unite in a true marriage, should express their love in universal friendship, and all the creative energies that are generated in their systems should be trans-muted into forces of ability, talent, genius and forces of personal expression. That is, their energies should be trained to develop extraordinary powers of mind, and a highly organized personality.

To transmute the creative energies of the system, attention should be directed upon the finer forces whenever creative energies are strongly felt in the system. These finer forces permeate every part of the system and act through the finer substance of the personality. To direct attention upon these finer forces and *desire to draw* all the creative energies of the system into the world of the finer forces will cause the creative energies to change their vibra-tions and begin to act in the field of the finer forces.

When the creative energies begin to act in the

field of the finer forces, the creative power of the personality will begin to express itself in every cell of body and brain, and development will be greatly promoted both in the mentality and the personality. In consequence, those forces that were simply perpetuating creative desire will begin to work for the re-creation of everything in the being of man.

To cause the creative energies to recreate the personality, the vibrations of those energies must be refined, because no force can be turned into a new creative channel until it is refined; that is, taken back into its original creative state. All creative energies proceed from the original creative state, therefore it is readily understood why they have to be drawn back to that state before they can proceed with creative work of another nature.

To take active creative energy back to its original state is called transmutation, and is promoted by *drawing* the active creative energy into the field of the finer forces. When this is done the new energies will follow the directions of desire; that is, all transmuted energy will immediately proceed to do what the mind at the time may desire to have done, though this desire must be strong, positive and clearly defined.

When the creative energy of the system has been transmuted, the mind, through its positive desire, may cause that energy to rebuild the entire personality; in this manner the creative energies may be trained to work in perfect harmony with the law of perpetual renewal, and as the transmuted energies are always finer than ordinary physical vitality, the personality will not only be constantly renewed but it will become a finer, a more highly developed and more highly organized personality every time that it has been renewed.

The actions of a strong, constant love will awaken all the creative energies that are latent in the system, and through the process of transmutation these energies can be turned into any channel in the human system where a higher development is desired. The desire, however, that is to govern these energies must have great depth of feeling and must invariably have higher attainments as its goal. And so long as these forces are rebuilding, recreating and refining the human system, old age is absolutely impossible.

To employ the power of love to the greatest possible advantage, the actions of love should be universal; that is, we should love everything and everybody in the largest, highest and most perfect sense, but in the expression of this complete love, the real alone should receive attention. The attitude of the true love is to ignore deficiencies; it gives thought only to the greatness and the divinity that constitute the real of everything, and to that which it gives thought it also gives love—all the love that can possibly be awakened in the fullness of heart and soul.

The great mind always loves much; in fact, no mind can become great unless it does love much. It is the power of love that awakens the powers of greatness, and these powers grow in greatness according to the greatness of the love. To increase the power of greatness it is therefore necessary to love more, but no mind can love more unless it begins to love everything, and no mind can love everything unless it transcends to the love of the soul.

To love everything with the love of the soul is to love the very best that exists in everything, because the soul invariably discerns the best; to love the best in everything is to give expression to the best of everything that exists in our natures, and to express the best that is within us is to outgrow the old and enter into the new. To enter the new always is to continue in the life of youth always, and this is what we do when we love always.

To promote the expression of the transcending soul love, there is no phase of the personal love that need be eliminated. All love is true love in its own sphere, but all love should be given expression, and that expression should be animated with the strongest and most tender feeling that the very soul of life can possibly awaken. The power of love should be expressed in all its fullness through every channel, but its tendency should ever be upward. The eyes of love should always be turned towards the beautiful, the ideal and the divine that we all have discerned in man's transcending nature. When we love persons and things we should love our highest idealizations of those persons and things, and when we love the ideal itself the mind should turn its vision upon the highest heights that our most sublime moments can possibly picture. The best, the truest and the most beautiful—that must be the goal of love.

When love loves as love is created to love, it is evident that youth must ever remain, because when the fires of love are ever at white heat, all the debris of age, weakness, decay, imperfection, disease and impurity will be completely consumed; and the personality of every person will ever be as clean, as young and as vigorous as that of the pure and wholesome child. The power of love will consume everything that is not as pure as love, and the same power will give the limitless life to everything because love is the *life* of all life.

When the being of man is spotless and clean through and through, and completely filled with the fullness of life, the elements of youth will develop in man in greater and greater measure; therefore, to love always is to be young always.

XVIII.

How to Live a Life That Will Perpetuate Youth.

To live a life that will perpetuate youth, the first essential is to die daily to the old; that is, everything that has served its purpose should be eliminated from the human system. To carry in the system anything that has served its purpose is to produce the aging tendency, because the accumulation of useless elements in the system will retard the renewing tendency.

That which has served its purpose, be it physical elements, mental states or ideas, can not be used anymore, and that which is of no use to the system will clog the system, thus interfering with every natural process. The accumulation of useless elements in mind or body will also produce ossification, because that which is not in use is not alive; it becomes dead matter, and such matter invariably withers, dries up and hardens every cell with which it comes in contact.

To die daily to the old, the mind must establish a subconscious eliminating process, because it is the subconscious that holds, and it is the subconscious that lets go. To die daily to the old is to live more in the new; therefore, to eliminate the old and the useless from the system, it is only necessary to train the subconscious to enter directly and constantly into the greater life of the new.

(160)

The natural way out of everything is to grow out, and to grow out of the old into the new is to eliminate the old without trying to do so. To try to eliminate the old is to practice resistance, and that which we continue to resist will continue to remain with us. We remove the lesser, the inferior, the imperfect by giving the whole of attention to the realization of the greater, the superior and the perfect.

To daily impress upon the subconscious a strong desire to grow into the new, will produce in the system a tendency to pass out of everything that has served its purpose, and enter into that which we can now use in promoting our greater purpose. This subconscious impression must be so deeply felt that every atom in the system is thoroughly animated with the same desire—the desire to retain only that now which can be of actual use now.

To die daily is to pass through a perpetual regenerative process, because to die, in the true sense of the term, is to eliminate the useless and transform to higher states of life and action those things that have permanent value in human advancement; and so long as regeneration is taking place in the system, the elements of youth will be perpetuated. The process of regeneration is a renewing process, a process that causes the human system to recreate itself in the likeness of higher and higher states of being, therefore, it is not possible for the personality to grow old while regeneration is taking place.

To live a life that will perpetuate youth, the first essential is to eliminate that which has served its purpose, and the second essential is to enter into that which can serve our greater purpose. That is, the first step is to die daily to the lesser life, and the second step is to live daily more and more in the greater life. These two essentials must be applied simultaneously and continually, because they are inter-dependent upon each other.

To enter daily into more and more life it is necessary to increase the inner consciousness of life, and this is accomplished by giving frequent attention to the finest life-vibrations that we can possibly picture throughout the system. When we try to realize more life it is the *living* element in the subconscious field that should receive attention, and as this element is realized to a degree, attention should be directed upon the *soul* of this living element. This process will take consciousness into the very depth of life itself, and the inner consciousness of life will increase constantly.

To increase the consciousness of life is to increase the power and action of life; the system will consequently become more and more alive, and it is not possible for old age conditions to enter the system so long as the aliveness is on the increase. It is the decrease of life that makes it possible for age and death to take place, therefore, so long as life is on the increase, the youth of the personality will positively be retained.

To live a life that will perpetuate youth, the mental attitude towards life must be in perfect accord with the purpose of life itself; that is, we must think of life as a power that naturally carries him

who lives into more and more life. Life is not a
burden but a power that removes all burdens and
produces absolute emancipation. To think of life as
a burden is to produce depressing conditions in the
system, and such conditions invariably produce old
age. Such thought will also retard the advancement
of life into more life—an advancement that is absolutely necessary to the perpetuation of youth.

The proper mental attitude towards life is to
approach life as something that lives more the more
it lives. To live properly is to live more; to live
more is to increase the power, the value and the joy
of life, and while these things are on the increase
the tendency to stay young will also be on the
increase.

To live more it is necessary to take an active interest, not only in life itself, but in everything that
is alive. To be thoroughly interested in life is to
mentally dwell with life, and the more closely we
live with life the more life we shall receive. To be
thoroughly interested in life is to advance into more
and more life because it is the nature of deep interest to advance into the larger domains of that upon
which the attention of interest is concentrated; therefore, a thorough interest in life will perpetually increase the power and volume of life, and youth will
not depart while such a life is being lived.

To be so deeply interested in life that every atom
thrills with the very *soul* of life, is to perpetually add
to the power of life; to increase this power is to
prevent all lack of life from ever taking place in any
part of the system; there will always be abund-

ance of life, and old age conditions can no more enter where there is abundance of life than darkness can enter where there is abundance of light.

The more we try to live, the more life we shall have to live. Supply is always equal to demand, and to face the limitless life with a strong, irresistible desire for limitless life, is to create a true demand for more life. The necessary supply will invariably follow.

To feel that life is a power that will carry us on and on towards the greater things and the greater heights, is to enter into the *soul* of this power, and it is when we are in the soul of life that we enter into the inner consciousness of more and more life. Thus we gain possession of an ever-growing abundance of that life that positively will perpetuate youth.

To live the life of youth in practical daily life, regardless of years, the conduct of the individual must be wholly determined by the present conditions of his own system. What a person can do, or what he can not do, depends not upon how many or how few years he has lived upon this planet; it is never a question of years, but a question of whether or not there are old age conditions in his system.

We must not deny others the privilege of doing what they are able to do, even though they have lived so long that those of similar years have no such ability. The man who can reach the century mark without having old age conditions in his system, has the privilege to do whatever the man of twenty-five has the privilege to do, because so long as there are no old age conditions in the system, the system is young and vigorous, and can do anything that any young and vigorous system can do.

Those who are competent have the privilege to do whatever the competent usually have the privilege to do, and years have no concern in the matter. To think that those who have lived three-quarters of a century or more, must not do certain things because they are "old" is to recognize age, and to recognize age in others is to produce old age conditions in ourselves.

What a person is to do, and what he is not to do must be determined wholly by power and ability. If the man of eighty has the same power and the same ability as the man of thirty, the former has the privilege to occupy the same positions as the latter in any sphere of life. If the man of a hundred or more is free from old age conditions, and he can be, he is still a young man, and may live the life of a young man. In fact he will be of far greater service to the world than men of fewer years because he has more experience.

We must deeply and positively impress upon our minds that many years do not produce age, weakness and uselessness. It is old age conditions that render the human system weak and useless, but old age conditions do not come from years; positively not; those conditions come from the violation of natural law, either in the mental or in the physical, or in both.

However, those who have produced in themselves old age conditions, must not think that they can now do what those can do who are free from old age conditions. The proper course to pursue is to first remove these old age conditions, and when this is done the normal vigor of youth will be regained.

We can do the work of youth only when we have the strength of youth, but we have not the strength of youth so long as our systems are full of old age conditions; nor will old age conditions disappear simply by our trying to do what youth alone is competent to do. We do not regain youth by trying to appear young, nor by trying to act as if we were young; we regain our youth by removing old age conditions, and these conditions any person can remove completely from his system.

The elimination of old age conditions, however, is a subconscious process, and will therefore not be affected by attempts to appear young and act as if you were young. When you remove old age conditions from the system you will be young through and through; you will consequently look young and act young without trying to do so. The power of youth comes from within; to enter more and more deeply into the inner consciousness of real life is to awaken this power, and when this power is awakened in the person, old age conditions will absolutely disappear, regardless of how many years that person may have lived.

XIX.

Regularity in All Things, Moderation in All Things.

To secure normal action among all the functions in the human system, perfect regularity in life, thought and conduct becomes absolutely necessary; and normal action throughout the system is indispensable to the perpetuation of youth. Regularity in all things must therefore become an inseparable part of personal existence, but the mind must not be placed in bondage to the present personal conception of regularity.

When the personal mind becomes so thoroughly impressed with the idea that it is necessary to be regular, even to the second, it becomes practically incapable of acting outside of its own self-created groove of regularity, and will consequently prevent its own enlargement and advancement. The mind, however, that goes to the other extreme, disregarding all regularity, will create for itself a mental world that is not only chaotic within itself, but that is also completely out of harmony with the laws and principles of life.

To find the happy mean in connection with the rules of regularity, the mind should be trained to think that you can do anything, but the body should do only what present capacity indicates that it can do, and what it does should be done in moderation.

The mind should be directed to expand constantly, to break bounds completely and to transcend its own laws, but the body should not be called upon to act outside of its regular channels until the mind has established itself in a greater mental world. When the mind is permanently established in a larger mental world, the capacity of the body will begin to increase, and the old rules are no longer necessary, but the capacity of the body will not increase until the mental world has actually been enlarged.

When a person simply thinks that he can do more than he does, and proceeds to use the body in that greater undertaking he fails, and the reason is found in the fact that the capacity of the human system does not increase the very moment we think we can do more. That he can who thinks he can is true, but it is true in this sense that he who continues to think that he can will develop the power that can.

To employ the faculties and the powers of the personality to their full capacity now, and then proceed to enlarge the mind, that is, to think that we can do more, is the proper course to pursue. To continue to enlarge the mind will cause the capacity of the personality to be enlarged, but the enlargement of the personal capacity is invariably an effect of the enlargement of the mental capacity. The enlargement of the mental capacity, however, is produced by scientific mental development, and does not follow the attempt to do more than we can do simply because we objectively think that we can.

When man thinks that he can, he awakens a great deal of latent energy, but that energy can not be used in constructive personal action until it is properly trained, and to promote this training, scientific mental development becomes necessary. To practically apply this principle, continue to think that you can do whatever you desire to do, but do not force your personality to do more than you feel that you can do. As the mind is enlarged, you will feel the increase of power and capacity, and will then be prepared to act upon a larger scale.

To properly observe the rules of regularity, the same principle should be employed; that is, the personality should be regular in all life and action, and thinking should be systematic, but the mind should aim to steadily transcend rules, methods and habits, and should gradually modify its modes of regularity as the needs of a constantly growing life might demand.

To scientifically apply the law of moderation, each individual must understand his own actual capacity, because to be moderate is to proceed to apply only as much life or power as you now have in actual possession. When a person attempts to do more than he now has the actual capacity to do, he becomes intemperate, and disturbs the normal conditions of the system. Likewise, when he attempts to eat or drink more than he can assimilate, or attempts to enjoy more than he has the present capacity to enjoy, he violates the law of moderation; he overstretches the functions of his system, and in consequence will bring adverse conditions upon himself.

There is nothing in existence that is actually bad; there is nothing that can do us harm unless we take too much of it or do too much of it; therefore, when the law of moderation is observed in all things, everything we do will prove beneficial.

The law of moderation, however, does not apply simply to those things in life that are now in action, but to everything in life that is created to be in action. Nothing should be overdone, neither should anything be underdone. To permit a faculty to lie dormant is a violation of the laws of life, just as much so as the intemperate use of that faculty. Everything in the human system should be placed in use, and in that use moderation should be observed.

When any part of the system is dormant, it merely exists; it is not alive; and that which is not alive will soon wither, dry up, ossify, decay and become "dead matter" in the system. Such matter will also tend to dry up and ossify other parts of the system with which it may come in contact, and age-producing tendencies will thus gain a foothold in the entire personality.

Those parts of the human system that are dormant are not growing; and that which is not growing is growing old. To perpetuate the qualities of youth it is therefore necessary to make the entire personality thoroughly alive, and to continue the full expression of the whole of that life. And this purpose may be promoted by causing every faculty, function and force in the system to continue in full normal action.

To place every function in full normal action, the force of every function should be used for some constructive purpose, and this becomes possible through the law of transmutation. When a function can not be constructively used in its usual line of action, the force of that function should be transmuted and applied in a different but kindred line of action. To place all the forces of the system so completely under the control of the mind that transmutation may take place at any time desired, the mind should frequently concentrate attention upon the subconscious side of every part of the personality, and should, during that concentration, place in the fullest possible action the finest forces at its command.

To give full, normal action to every function in the system, both the mental life and the physical life must be given the best of scientific care. Every impression that enters the mind should be wholesome; in like manner, everything that enters the body should be wholesome, but we should fear nothing. A special system of diet is not necessary, nor do we require extensive systems of physical and mental gymnastics, but we should give all these matters the best attention possible.

To eat anything, drink anything, do anything, and call it all good, is not scientific. Things are what they are whether we call them this or that, nevertheless, our mental attitude towards things will modify, to a great degree, the natural effects that those things have the power to produce. To be scientific, we should select the best of everything in the physical world and combine that best with our best thought; then we shall secure the best effects both from the physical and the mental sides of life, and that is our object in view.

To be reckless in our eating and drinking and living, and then expect to neutralize undesirable effects with the power of thought is to waste energy, but no person who is wasting his energy can stay young. To stay young it is not only necessary to retain the energy we now possess, but it is also necessary to constantly increase the power of that energy. And this is readily accomplished when we live scientifically and aim to so live that we are eternally living more.

To perpetuate the qualities of youth, all the requirements of the human system must be supplied, and to this end both the mind and the body must be well fed, but neither should be over fed. The entire system should be well exercised, but no exercise should become mechanical. To give mental interest and soul to every form of exercise is necessary, because otherwise the exercise becomes mechanical, and mechanical exercise is wearing to the system; it never develops; it never increases power but always uses up power; it is never beneficial but is always detrimental.

The body requires a fresh, physical atmosphere; in like manner, the mind requires a fresh mental

atmosphere. To breathe dead air is to weaken the
life of the system, and when the power of life begins to decrease the power of youth will begin to
decrease also; but to think dead thought is to produce the same effect. To live in a dead, fixed,
changeless, motionless, stereotyped mental atmosphere is one of the shortest of paths to uselessness
and old age; nevertheless, it is in this sort of mental atmosphere that the great majority live.

To perpetuate the qualities of youth, everything
that is appropriated by the human system in any
shape or form, must contain the spirit of youth;
that is, it must be fresh from the great creative
power; it must be new, and it must be wholesome
to the highest possible degree. And when the laws
of regularity and moderation are applied in the use
of all these things, that which contains the elements
of youth will invariably give expression to the life
of youth. In consequence, man will continue to
stay young.

XX.

The Rejuvenating Power of Sleep When Properly Slept.

When the conscious ego goes to sleep it enters the subconscious, and in doing so has two objects in view. The first object is to carry into the basic mentality the results of the day's experience, and the second is to receive a new supply of life-force with which to recharge the personality upon awakening.

The nature and the actions of the subconscious mind determine the conditions of the objective mind and the physical body, and since everything that enters the subconscious will affect its nature and actions, it is highly important that the conscious ego, when it is going to sleep, conveys to the subconscious only those things that will promote the purpose that the individual may have in view.

The conditions of old age originate in the subconscious; the same is true of the qualities of youth; but what is to originate in the subconscious is determined principally by what the conscious ego carries into the within when going to sleep, therefore, the art of staying young depends to a very great extent upon the art of going to sleep.

What is taken into the subconscious becomes a part of the nature of the individual, but the conscious ego can, before going to sleep, eliminate those things that will prove detrimental to the health, the youth

(174)

and the welfare of the individual, and in doing so may determine absolutely the future conditions of the personality. The time of going to sleep is the sowing time; at this time we may sow what we like, and what we sow we shall reap.

To sleep properly is to enter the subconscious with those impressions, ideas and desires only that we wish to have reproduced in mind and body. To sleep well is to reconstruct the entire subconscious mentality according to a higher, larger and more perfect mental conception, and to do so in a state of peace, harmony and sweet repose. To awaken from a refreshing sleep is to awaken in the consciousness of that state of mind that invariably follows the complete renewal of the subconscious mind, and the renewal of the subconscious always takes place during sleep when we go to sleep with mind in the upper story.

To go to sleep with the mind in the upper story is to carry into the subconscious only those impressions that have a constructive tendency; in consequence, the subconscious will in the morning, be superior in comparison to what it was the evening before. It is therefore evident that if the mind is in the upper story every night when it goes to sleep, the subconscious mind will, in the course of months or years, become highly developed through this process alone, and as the subconscious is, so is also the entire personality.

To place the mind in the upper story before going to sleep, the entire attention should be subjectively concentrated, for a few moments, upon the highest conceptions of our ideals that we can possibly form, and during this concentration, consciousness 'should actually rise into the superior states of the upper region of mentality. In this upper region the mind will find that peace, that harmony, that sweet repose and that unspeakable delight that makes true existence so rich and beautiful; and what the mind finds in this upper region will be taken into the subconscious to be later made a part of the whole man.

When the mind goes to sleep in the lower story, all the worries, disappointments, mistakes, confusions, ill-feelings, misconceptions and troubled thoughts that have formed during the day, will be carried into the subconscious; in consequence, the subconscious field will bring forth a harvest of tares, such as sickness, trouble, poverty, adversity, weakness and aging conditions; and if the mind goes to sleep every night, or nearly every night, in this manner, the subconscious will steadily become more and more inferior until its entire power is gone. Then the personality can no longer exist, and the end will speedily follow.

The reason why the average person begins to go down after a period of thirty or forty years have been passed, is due to several causes, all of which have been mentioned except one; and that one is found in the fact that the subconscious is made weaker and more inferior every year because the conscious ego usually goes to sleep in the lower story. In the earlier years of the average person, responsibilities are few, but after the age of twenty-five or thirty these responsibilities begin to multiply, and to the average mind they feel like burdens. With these burdens the mind goes to sleep and the subconscious is weakened thereby. In consequence, the personality will begin to go down in health, capacity, power, ambition, vigor and life; growth will cease, and when growth ceases, old age begins.

The responsibilities of life should not be looked upon as burdens; they are never burdensome so long as we live for the purpose of turning all things to good account, and we shall gain the power to turn all things to good account when we continue to develop the subconscious. To accomplish this, the difficulties, the obstacles and the adversities we have met during the day must be eliminated from conscious attention before we go to sleep. To build a superior subconscious mentality, the superior only must be taken into the subconscious, and this is done by giving the whole of attention to our highest conceptions of the ideal, the worthy and the superior as we are going to sleep. That is, we should enter the upper story of mind for some time, an hour or two if possible, before going to sleep, and we should take that superior state of consciousness with us into the great within.

When we go to sleep in this manner, the quality, the life and the power of the subconscious will be constantly increased and improved; the entire personality will consequently advance, and so long as the personality continues to advance it will continue to stay young. However, to go to sleep in the usual way is to cause the subconscious to go down to weakness and inferiority, and old age will positively follow such conditions. The great majority go to sleep with their minds in the lower story, but it is not possible to stay young unless we habitually go to sleep in the upper story.

To perpetuate the youth of the personality, the subconscious life must be perpetually developed, because youth is inseparable from growth, and all growth originates in a growing subconscious life. But to go to sleep in the lower story of mind is to take into the subconscious those conditions of thought and experience that will retard growth, while to go to sleep with the mind in the upper story is to impress upon the subconscious the superior only, that which has constructive power, that which tends to build for greater things. It is, therefore, evident that to go to sleep with the mind in the upper story is absolutely necessary if the qualities of youth are to be retained.

When we go to sleep properly, we always feel rejuvenated upon awakening; the mind is new, consciousness is refreshed, the body feels thoroughly recuperated, and the entire personality is recharged with life, strength and vigor. We feel young, because we are young; we have been supplied once more with the elements of youth, and should begin the day in the conviction that we do possess the ability, the quality and the power of youth.

When we go to sleep we should enter the subconscious with the idea clearly fixed in mind that we are young; and upon awakening we should impress the same idea upon every atom in the system. To enter the subconscious in the full conviction that we have the life and the vigor of youth, is to cause the subconscious to give forth into the personality a greater measure of that power that does produce youth. In consequence, the personality will feel young, look young and actually *be* young, regardless of years.

To begin the day with the conviction that we do possess the life and the vigor of youth, is to continue in the youth producing attitude during that day; ere long it will become second nature to spend the waking state in the youth producing attitude, and he who lives every day in the youth producing attitude will perpetually produce youth in his own system, therefore he will continue to stay young.

To secure the best results from sleep, seven or eight hours out of every twenty-four should be taken for sleep; but never less than six nor more than nine; to secure insufficient sleep is to secure insufficient life, because all life-force comes from within, and to take too much sleep is to stupefy the mind. When the energies of the system are not placed in constructive action the very hour the system is fully recharged, their desire for action will express itself in mere desire, and to desire to act without having the opportunity to act is to waste power. Therefore, important work should be undertaken at once in the morning; this method will produce better work, and when night comes again it will be a matter of perfect ease to go to sleep in the upper story.

XXI.

The Necessity of Perfect Health and How to Secure It.

To perpetuate the youth of the personality, perfect and continuous health becomes an absolute necessity, but this condition is not difficult to secure because the human system has within itself the power to supply itself with a full measure of absolute health so long as it may exist as an organized form.

There is an element of health in every atom in the being of man, and this element when in action has the power to give perfect health to the entire atom; therefore, the secret of perfect health is to give continuous action to all the elements of health throughout the human system, and this may be accomplished in various ways but there is one best way.

Whenever any system of medication succeeds in healing the body, results are due to the fact that the elements of health that are latent in the system were placed in action by the methods employed. There is only one power that can remove disease, and that power is the power of health that is already latent in the life of the human system. To arouse that power is to heal, and any method

(180)

through which that power may be aroused, may be used successfully in the cure of disease.

To secure the best results, the system of therapeutics that is employed should not be used for the purpose of combating disease, but should be used directly for the purpose of giving greater activity to the power of health that exists in the life of the human personality. When diseased conditions gain a foothold in the body, the normal action of the power of health is interfered with; in fact, a disease is simply something that interferes with the normal action of the power of health, and it has entered the system because the power of health was permitted to run low.

The only scientific method of cure, therefore, is to increase the power of health. To apply this method the first essential is to learn why the power of health was permitted to run low, and the cause will usually be found in an adverse mental attitude. The immediate cause of low vitality in the system is produced by reckless or ignorant waste of energy, and this waste is invariably brought about by the false attitude of the mind towards that something, in connection with which, the energy was applied.

When energy is wasted in connection with work the cause is due to the fact that that work was not properly approached; that is, the work was not taken up in the right attitude. To think of work as wearing and tearing, or as wearisome drudgery, is to work in the wrong attitude; in consequence, energy will be wasted; but when every action applied in work is subjectively recognized as an action of development, every action exercised in work will promote development.

The actions of the personality will do what we direct them to do. When we firmly believe that work uses up energy, every action expressed in work will use up energy, but when we know that every action can place more and more power in action, and work with that object in view, work will become exercise. Such work will not use up energy, but will, instead, increase the supply of energy.

The attitude towards pleasure will, in like manner, increase or decrease the vitality of the system, depending upon the nature of the attitude entered into at the time. To enter pleasure for mere personal gratification is to waste energy and reduce to a minimum the joy expected; but to enter pleasure for the purpose of gaining the *soul* of enjoyment is to place the mind in touch with the finer elements of life; in consequence, new life will be gained and the maximum of joy secured.

The mental attitudes towards life, action, thought and living in general, will, through the same principle, determine whether life-force is to be decreased or increased; therefore, the first essential in the attainment of health is to place the mind in those attitudes where power is never wasted, but instead, is constantly being accumulated.

The attitudes of accumulation mentally face the limitless at all times, and their object in view is to act in conscious touch with the *soul* of all things.

When the mind enters into every action with the purpose of unfolding the *soul* of that action it is in the right attitude providing it subjectively recognizes the *soul* as the open way to limitless life and power.

To give subjective recognition to any idea, law or principle, is to place the mind in the *finer feeling* of life and action while that recognition is active in consciousness, and the power to do this is extremely valuable, because subjective action is back of all physical action; therefore, any physical action or change may be secured when the corresponding subjective action can be produced.

To produce any desired subjective change, place the mind in the *finer feeling* of life, and mentally picture the change as you would wish to see it in reality. Through this simple process, the subconscious mind is directed to do what you desire to have done, and whatever the subconscious is directed to do it positively will do.

The second essential in the attainment of health is to give greater action to the power of health that is latent in every part of the system, and the first step to be taken in this connection is to convince the intellect that the human system has the power to generate its own health. If the system did not have such a power, it would not be possible for the body to regain perfect health through the recuperative powers of the body alone, but the fact that it is nature alone that can heal, proves conclusively that nature has the real secret to health.

The value of systems of therapeutics is to be

found only in their power to place in action nature's healing agency, and the best of these systems
is the metaphysical system. Chemical systems do
not always reach the inner conditions of things,
that is, the bottom cause, but metaphysics, when
intelligently applied, can reach the very foundation
of the trouble and remove it.

To actually know and to mentally feel that the
human system has the power to generate its own
health, opens the way perfectly for the application
of metaphysics, and to secure this inner conviction
of the reality of health all that is necessary is to
reason logically about nature and her recuperative
power. Those, however, who already have perfect
health can, during their serene moments of thought,
actually feel the elements of absolute health per-
meating every part of the system.

When the power of health is felt in this manner,
the consciousness of absolute health has begun, and
to steadily develop this consciousness is highly important because whatever we become conscious of
we invariably bring forth into tangible expression.
To deepen and develop the consciousness of absolute health will therefore cause a larger measure of
health and a higher degree of health to find constant expression in the physical form.

When the mind has become convinced, either
through logical conclusions or conscious realizations, that the elements of perfect health do exist
in every part of the body, and that these elements
have the power to give perfect health to the entire
physical body so long as it may exist in organized

form, steps may be taken to place these elements of health in full, positive action.

To proceed, the mind should first give subjective recognition to the existence of the elements of health in every part of the system. This will place the actions of mind in perfect touch with these elements so that whenever the mind may act upon the elements of health, they will readily respond. To be able to place the elements of health in greater action when required is to have an infallible remedy constantly at hand.

To give action to the elements of health, the subconscious life of those elements must first be acted upon because every action must proceed from the subconscious. To act upon the subconscious of these elements, the mind should direct attention upon what may be termed the *soul* of health, and should, at the time, desire, with the deepest soul of desire the full realization of the soul of health. This action of mind will take consciousness into the very depths of the reality of health, and in consequence will produce a larger expression of real health.

The subconscious mind in general, should also be frequently impressed with the idea of perfect health, and the statement, "I am well," should be made a living power in subconscious thought: In addition, thinking in general should conform absolutely to the principle that the reality of the being of man always is well. Neither word nor thought should ever contradict the great truth that the real man is always well, nor should the individual ever think of himself as being anything else but the real man.

To live perpetually in the consciousness of the reality of life, health and wholeness is to permanently establish the active power of real health in the subconscious, and this is our object in view. There is an abundance of latent health in the system, and what we aim to do is to place that health in action; but this action must be subconscious or it will not be permanent.

When the health of the subconscious life is being placed in action to a greater and a greater degree, the tangible elements of health will begin to express themselves in the body to the same degree; and if this process is continued progressively, the normal health of the body will be increased perpetually, thus providing the greater supply of health that will naturally be demanded by the increasing capacity of an ever advancing life.

To be simply well is not sufficient; continuous advancement is the law of life, and to be in harmony with life everything must advance with life; therefore, both the quality and the power of health must be increased perpetually. To be satisfied with simply having good health, is to begin to lose health, because that which ceases to move forward will begin to move backward. To prevent the losing of health, it is necessary to develop better and better health.

When an ailment appears in any part of the body, the mind should at once concentrate attention upon the elements of health in that part where the ailment has its actual origin; this concentration, however, should be subjective, because subjective concentration invariably gives action to that upon which the concentration is directed.

To give action to the elements of health wherever the ailment may appear, is to cause that ailment to completely disappear. When the ailment is of recent origin a complete cure may be secured almost at once, and chronic ailments may be removed in the course of a few weeks, frequently in much less time. There is no malady, however, that is incurable; the power of health in the system is greater than any disease, because the former is natural, while the latter is unnatural; therefore, perseverance will invariably succeed.

The elements of health should be given greater action, also, in those parts that are in good health; first, because the increase of health in the whole body will make it easier to remove an ailment from any part of the body, and second, because to always have good health we must constantly develop better and better health.

XXII.

Live in the Conviction That it is Natural to Stay Young.

The purpose of life is continuous advancement; all the principles of life are based upon that purpose and all the laws of life are formed to promote that purpose. Everything in nature is created with an inherent tendency to advance, to move forward, to rise in the scale, therefore anything that retards continuous advancement or that is not in harmony with continuous advancement is unnatural, and that which is unnatural is caused by a violation of natural law.

To promote continuous advancement in the being of man is to cause every element, force, function, faculty and action in the human system to rise perpetually in the scale of life; this means increased activity, a higher order of activity with greater results from every human endeavor; but such results can not be secured if the system is permitted to go down to weakness and old age. To grow old is to go in the opposite direction; it is to retard all progress and to decrease both the quality and the quantity of those results that naturally follow the actions of life. To grow old, therefore, is unnatural a direct violation of the laws of life.

To act in harmony with the laws of life, the in-

(188)

dividual must move forward perpetually, but when he permits himself to grow old he does not move forward; instead, he causes everything in his system to go down; it is therefore evident that the aging process is contrary to the purpose of life, and is not a product of nature. Since it is unnatural to grow old it must be natural to stay young; in consequence, every person, to be true to nature, must not only live in the full conviction that it is natural to stay young, but he must so live that he perpetually will stay young.

That perpetual youth is a gift of nature is evident to all who will search the real life of nature, but only those who are true to nature can receive the gift. To be true to nature, the individual must not only live in harmony with the laws of nature, but must also aim to become as much as nature has given him the power to become. Nature has given man the power to advance perpetually, and has given him unlimited possibilities through which such advancement may be promoted; therefore, to be true to his nature man must take advantage of the privilege that has been placed in his possession.

To live in the conviction that it is natural to stay young, is to base all life, all thought and all action upon that conviction, and consequently everything that is said or done must be in harmony with the idea of staying young. To be in harmony with this idea a number of usual statements, plans and intentions must be changed completely. We must no longer say, "the older I get," but should say instead, "the longer I live." To use the first statement is to cause the mind to think that old age is actually coming on, and such thought will invariably produce the aging tendency. To use the second statement is to ignore age and impress upon the mind the idea of a longer and a longer life.

To live in harmony with the idea of youth, we must never think of saving for old age, because such thought will cause the mind to look forward to old age, to expect age, and consequently to produce age. Instead, we should think of accumulating for use in a larger future. To live in the thought of accumulation will cause all the forces of life to produce perpetual increase in our own world, and to constantly look forward to a larger future will cause these same forces to create for us a larger future.

To think of saving for a rainy day, is in like manner, thoroughly unscientific. To expect rainy days is to produce hard luck, and to live in the belief that we may be in dire need sometime, is to limit our own powers more and more until their capacity to produce the necessary supply is practically reduced to nothing.

To be scientific we should continue to accumulate in the present in order that we may have abundance in the coming days, and thus be able to take advantage of those greater opportunities that positively will come to him who lives the advancing life. To be natural we must expect to stay young, and to continue to stay young is to continue to live an active, useful, productive life. Such a life will naturally enter into larger and larger fields of endeavor, and to take the best possible advantage of those larger fields we must accumulate the best of everything in the present.

We must not, however, deal penuriously with the present; everything that can be used to advantage now should be placed in use now; nothing should be hoarded in the present that can, if placed in use, produce increase in the present, but we should never try to save and accumulate in the present because we expect want in the future. There will be no want in the future if we make the best possible use of our faculties in the present, but the future will present larger opportunities, and we do not wish to approach those opportunities empty handed.

To live more thoroughly and more completely in the conviction that it is natural to stay young, the statement, "I am young," should be frequently impressed upon the mind; in fact, the whole life should live and move and have its being in the very spirit of that statement. To live in the real spirit of youth is to absolutely know that we are in the life of youth; that is, we will know the great truth that real life is ever young, and the knowing of that truth will place the entire system in that life. It is this truth that will give us freedom from the falseness of old age and place being in the true state of youth, vigor, health and wholeness.

When we know that real life is ever young, it becomes second nature to live in the conviction that it is natural to stay young, because only that which is real is natural; and what becomes second nature becomes subconscious. To stay young will therefore become an inseparable part of life, due to the fact that as the subconscious is, so is also the entire person of man.

To live in the conviction that it is natural to stay young, it is necessary to train consciousness to enter as deeply as possible into the *soul* of nature; on the surface, nature may suggest varying ideas, but in the depth of the *soul* of nature the ideas of continuous advancement and continuous youth are revealed in most positive terms; and it is not appearances, but the real truth, upon which we must base our convictions.

When the mind realizes absolutely that it is natural to stay young, the forces of human nature will begin to produce youth; they will cease to follow unnatural race habits, and will, instead, proceed to do what they were created to do. The entire human system will be emancipated from the false thought of the ages, and will be placed absolutely in the keeping of real life itself. In consequence, the purpose of life—continuous advancement—will be promoted in the life of man; and from continuous advancement, continuous youth must invariably follow.

To move forward is to stay young; and since it is natural to move forward, it is natural to stay young; therefore, there is no old age in store for him who fulfills the natural purpose of life by living the life of continuous advancement. To him, the future is a bright picture of youth, ever becoming larger, more beautiful and more ideal.

To know life—the soul of life, is to know that real life is ever young; and he who lives life grows into the likeness of the life he lives; it is therefore evident that he who continues to live real life will continue to stay young as long as he lives. And real life is eternal.

XXIII.

What To Do With Birthdays.

The number of years that a person has lived upon this planet is not important, but it is extremely important to place the mind in the proper attitude towards the idea of years, especially that idea that takes birthdays for its nucleus. To the average person, birthdays and the process of growing old are inseparably united, and for that reason the usual thought about birthdays is an age-producing thought; but in reality, birthdays are in no manner connected with the aging process, therefore the entire subject must be viewed under new light.

When a person declares that he is thus or so old, he is not speaking the truth, because age is a false condition, not a product of years. It is a scientific fact that years are wholly incapable of producing any condition of age in the person, therefore birthdays and age can have no connection whatever.

To be scientific, the individual must never think of himself as being so many years old, because such a thought will cause the mind to expect every year to increase the conditions of age; years, however, can not produce age, but thought can, and the thought that expects age will produce age. The two words "years" and "old", should therefore never be combined in the same sentence. They are contradictions, and will not mix.

To think of age at all is wrong, because in the right there is no age; what we call age is simply a mistake, and should be forgotten. The individual, however, may, with perfect propriety, state how many years he has lived in his present personal life, because it is the truth that he has lived as many years as he has lived, but it is not the truth that those years have produced age.

When the birthdays arrive, the mind should be deeply impressed with the idea that another step in the ascending life has been taken; a birthday should be looked upon as a mark of progress, because in the true, advancing life, that is what it is. When we live the life of continuous advancement, every birthday will indicate that we are, not so much older, but so much higher in the scale of the life beautiful.

The true birthday is celebrated by the individual proving to himself that he has actually taken another step; that he is more vigorous in body, more youthful in appearance, more perfect in personality, more brilliant in mind and more beautiful in soul.

When you celebrate your birthday, do not think of yourself as being a year older, a year nearer age, uselessness, death and the grave; such ideas should be banished forever; but think of yourself as being a step nearer the greater life, the superior life, the beautiful life, the ideal life—the fair, transcendent goal that you so often have seen during those sublime moments when the soul was revealed to your vision.

There is a great goal that every person has in

view; on the path towards this goal there are many ambitions to be perfected, many desires to be fulfilled, many ideals to be realized, many dreams to be made true, and after all of these come the goal itself. To live the true, advancing life is to move forward towards this great goal, realizing one ideal after another, until every wish of the heart has been granted; and every birthday will mark the great good gained during the year that has just been fulfilled.

To associate birthdays with the advancement of life is to look forward to every birthday as the realization of a greater measure of the richness of life, and what we constantly expect we invariably produce.

To think of the coming birthday as a realization of more of everything that we have lived for and worked for, is to cause all the forces of life to work together to make all our wishes come true when the next birthday arrives; and to think of every birthday as the beginning of a new life—a life of higher attainments and greater achievements than we have ever realized before, is to cause all the forces of life to proceed to make this greater dream also come true.

When years are considered in connection with birthdays, always state that you are so many years young; and it is the truth; you are not so many years old because you are not old; there is no age in real life; but you are so many years young because you have lived so many years, and during those years you have continued to stay young.

There may be old age conditions in your system, but they do not belong to you; they were not produced by the years you have lived; they are mere mistakes, and will disappear when you take the firm stand that you *are* young, because nature has placed the gift of youth in the actual possession of every man.

When you desire to learn the number of years that others have lived always ask "how young are you?" or "how many years have you lived?" but do not even think of age; such thought has no place whatever in a scientific mind. Never hesitate to state how young you are; always give the exact number of years when requested to do so; prevarications are not conducive to perpetual youth. To try to hide the number of years you have lived, is to produce a subconscious fear of age, and to fear age is to produce age.

The idea that we can retard the oncoming of age by stating positively that we are eighteen, twenty-two or twenty-seven, when we have lived two or three times as many years, has no foundation in exact science; besides such statements are never true in any sense, and to impress untruth upon the subconscious is to form a tendency in the subconscious to unconsciously accept the untruth; in consequence, we shall be misled in a thousand ways.

To state the exact number of years you have lived, when requested to do so, is scientific, and is in harmony with those laws through which you may perpetuate your youth, but only those who have a personal interest in your life, or who have legal matters to arrange for you, have the privilege to ask how many years you have lived. To ask such a question for mere curiosity is not conducive to youth, because those who ask such questions out of curiosity are thinking of age, not of youth; they therefore bring age upon themselves through their own misdirected inquisitiveness.

The number of years that a person has lived is of secondary importance, and should be thought of as such, nevertheless, no person should try to deceive himself or others in this respect. To be scientific, you should be proud of your years, and you should glory in the fuller life, the larger mentality, the greater power and the more vigorous youth that those years have produced. And these are the results that will invariably follow the coming of more and more years, when we constantly live the advancing life.

When every year is looked upon as an opportunity to add to the power, the richness and the joy of life, and that opportunity is taken advantage of, every year will produce the greater power, the greater richness and the greater joy; the many years will produce a greater measure of the same desirable results, therefore, we may well be proud of the years we have lived; we will have good reason to glory in the fact that we have lived long because we have lived exceedingly well.

To him who lives the true life, the coming of more years will bring more vigorous youth; he will daily pass from the youth of incompleteness to the

youth of high development; he will continue to
stay young, but every year will give his youth
greater power, greater capacity, a more perfect
personality, and a superior mind. To him, every
year is a rising path, and every birthday the reaching of greater heights than he has ever reached
before.

To speak of anything as old is unscientific, because nothing that is of permanent value can grow
old, and that which is not of permanent value should
not be mentioned. The great products of the race,
such as music, art, literature, invention, scientific
facts, lofty, ideals—these can never grow old; they
have the same power now as when they first
appeared, and that same power they will continue
to possess for countless ages yet to be. They are
as young now as when they were born; they are
products of real life, therefore theirs is the life of
eternal youth.

To speak of the old songs, the old writers, the
old composers, the old philosophers, the old masters—all of that is a false conception of life. To
think of anything as old because it first existed in
the years gone by, is to think of age and years as
synonymous, and this is the very idea we positively must eliminate.

To think of time as the great eternal now—
beginningless and endless—and to think that everything that was, now is, and evermore shall be—this
is the thought of exact science. To him who thinks
of life in this manner, all things are eternal, and
that which is eternal will never grow old. To such

a mind the spirit of youth reigns supremely throughout the universe, and in that spirit he lives; therefore, the life that he lives will be the life of youth—
eternal youth. To him, every birthday will be the
birth of a new day—a more glorious day than he has
ever beheld before.

XXIV.

How Long We May Live Upon Earth.

The greatest thing that man can do is to live the largest life, the best life, the happiest life and the most useful life in the great eternal now. To think of time is unscientific, and to fix any special length of time for existence on this planet is to shorten the period of that existence.

The proper course to pursue is to live so well every moment that that moment is absolutely complete in itself; and he who lives well will live long; in fact, how long we are to live upon earth depends upon how well we live upon earth. So long as the present moment is constructive, the power of life will increase during the present moment, and so long as we can increase the life-power of our present state of existence we will continue to live in our present state of existence.

To live well is to live more, and to live more is to live longer. To live well, it is necessary to concentrate the whole of attention upon life, upon the largest life, the best life, the greatest life and the most perfect life that the mind can possibly picture. The thought of death must never enter consciousness, nor must any fixed period of time for living upon earth be formed in mind. To *live* now must be the purpose, and he who actually lives now, thinks only of the abundance of life and the

(201)

richness of life that he can give to the life that he lives now.

It is the purpose of life to live, and to fulfill that purpose it is necessary to give our undivided attention to life. To think of death as well as life, is to divide attention; in consequence, the force of life is decreased; life is not lived so well; we fail to receive from life what life has to give; we limit the power of personal existence in every form and manner, and therefore shorten our days upon earth.

To impress upon mind the belief that you will live upon earth for a special period of time, is to place limitations upon the power of life, and the forces of life will consequently work for a temporal personal existence. Such thought will also produce aging conditions in the system, because to expect to get old some time is to think of old-age conditions, and to think of old-age conditions now is to create those conditions now.

Whether we expect to live a hundred years or a thousand years, the results will be the same; to fix a time now is to expect age and death, and to expect those things is to give life, power and thought to the producing of those things; therefore to think of future age and death is to produce aging conditions and decaying conditions in the system now. The man who expects to live a thousand years will, subconsciously, think just as much of age and death as the man who expects to live only three score and ten; both will produce old age conditions in their systems now, and both, on account of old age, may be forced to retire from active life at sixty.

To impress any time limit upon mind in regard to how many years we may live upon earth is always a mistake; to limit the mind at all is to weaken the power of life, and to weaken the power of life now is to begin to go down to age and death now. The proper course is never to think of how long we may live upon earth, but to live now in the consciousness of eternal life.

The purpose of life is not how long in any place, but how well in every place. We are here to live until we have fulfilled that purpose for which we came here to live; how many years it may require any individual to fulfill his purpose will depend upon how well he lives while he does live, therefore he can fix no time for himself; he can only proceed to live now the greatest life that he possibly can live now.

To remain upon this planet after we have fulfilled the purpose for which we came, is not according to the laws of eternal life; we will depart sometime; there are other mansions in which the soul is destined to dwell, but when we are to take our departure does not concern us now. We are not here to think of a future life, to live for a future life, or to work for a future life; we are here to think, live and work for this present state of existence—to give all the powers of being to the life we are living now.

When we analyze the purpose and the possibilities of this present existence, we come invariably to the conclusion that the period that the average person lives upon earth is far too short to even fulfill a small fraction of the purpose for which he came; but he must not think, however, that life is too short. To think that life is too short is to make it too short, while to realize that life is eternal, and that we may secure from the boundless, all the life we may desire to live, is to make life as long and as large as we may wish it to be.

The life of the average person is shortened by mistakes, most of which he has inherited from the race, but he can eliminate those mistakes, and when he does, he will find that the capacity of the human personality to extend its organized existence is marvelous indeed. To continue only for one short month to preserve all the energy that is generated in the system is to become so enormously strong, both in personality and mentality, that the mind feels as if the power *that moves mountains* has actually been gained. It is therefore evident that if the individual continued, not only to preserve his energy, but also to increase his energy, the organized existence of the personality could be perpetuated for an indefinite period, or until the purpose of life in this sphere had been fulfilled.

The power of any organized form to perpetuate its own existence, is far greater than the average mind has heretofore realized; in fact, nature gives every organized form the inherent power to perpetuate its own life until the purpose of that life has been completed; therefore, it is not natural for anything to pass away until it has finished its work in this sphere. When anything leaves its work unfinished, some natural law has been violated. No one in particular may be to blame, and there will be an opportunity to make amends, but there is one great truth to be remembered in this connection; it is this, that if we fail to fulfill the purpose of our present existence now, we will have to work out that purpose in the future. Where that is to happen is not germane to this study, but it must be done before we can rise in the scale. We must take the first step before we can take the second; we must complete the lesser that is at hand before we can inherit the greater that is in store.

This fact will prove conclusively to any mind that nothing is gained by wasting the present moment, and that nothing can give greater gain to any individual than to make the *living of life* the greatest aim of life. We are not here by chance; there is no chance; we came here because this present life has something in store for us—something that can add to the splendor of eternal existence. And when we have found this something we may rise to greater heights where other treasures are in store—treasures that are richer by far than anything we have ever known before.

The pathway of life is eternal progress, perpetual ascension towards the spiritual heights of the soul's transcendent existence, but the glory of real life is not deferred until some faraway future time. The ascending life is full and complete every moment; all that the present moment can hold, the present moment will receive, so long as life is rising in the scale, and in that *all* will be found the best of everything that the heart may desire now.

To live the ascending life is to live now for the perpetual ascension of life now, giving no thought whatever to the future; he who lives such a life will continue to live upon earth until the purpose for which he came has been fulfilled; and he will continue in the full vigor of youth as long as he lives. To live the ascending life is to produce a perpetual increase in life, and so long as man continues to increase his life he will not only continue to live in personal form, but that personal form will continue to stay young.

To live upon this planet until our work here is finished, until we have learned all that is here to be learned, until we have attained all that is here to be attained, until we have received all that is here to be received, until we have done all that is here to be done, until we have given all that is here to be given, until we have reached the highest heights that are here to be found—this is our purpose; and we must live in the conviction that we have sufficient life within us to live in vigor, strength, youth, health and wholeness until that great goal has been reached.

We must never stop, however, to think "how long"; how long we may live upon earth is a question we must never try to answer; if we are true to life we may live here as long as there is anything here to live for; and when we begin to really live we shall find so much here to live for that all thought of taking our departure will have completely disappeared. When we shall have reached the supreme heights of this present life, then, and not until then, shall we turn our spiritual vision upon the path to another world.

There is one truth, however, that will soon demonstrate itself conclusively to those who have chosen to be true to life, and it is this, that we may, under present circumstances and conditions, live several times as long as the average person has usually lived; also, that through the advancement of our own circumstances and conditions, we may go beyond that period and prolong life indefinitely, or until we have finished that for which we came; and from that long and beautiful life, neither youth nor happiness will ever depart.

XXV.

A New Picture of the Coming Years.

The life that is lived exclusively for the great eternal now does not necessarily confine its whole attention to the present moment. Such a life is constantly moving forward, and to move forward is to look forward. To look forward is to form pictures of the coming days, and since the nature of these pictures will determine what the life of the coming days is to be, the entire power of exact science may be applied most profitably in this art of picturing the future.

What is pictured in the mind the life-forces will produce, and every condition that is constantly expected during a life-time will positively be realized. The average person, however, expects age, physical and mental decline, and everything that inevitably follows such conditions; and he receives what he expects to receive. The picture that he has formed of the coming days contains nearly every undesirable condition that human life has known, and he lives, during his entire personal existence, in the deep subconscious conviction that the details of that picture constitute his future fate. But such thought is wholly adverse to the nature and the purpose of life, therefore, to be true to life we must form a new picture of the coming years.

The new picture will form itself naturally and perfectly in the mind that has accepted the new conception of life, that is, that conception that conceives of life as a path of eternal progress, an existence of continuous advancement and a state of perpetual increase in everything that can add to the worth, the welfare and the happiness of man. This new conception reverses practically everything that we have believed before, and as man is as he thinks, it is but natural that this new conception should give him a future that is practically the reverse of what has been expected and realized before.

The new picture of the coming years is ideal in the very highest sense of that term, but all ideals that are in harmony with the nature and purpose of life can be realized; and as this picture is such an ideal we may proceed to work it out with the full conviction that every part of it will come to pass.

To gain the realization of an ideal that is in harmony with the nature and the purpose of life, the secret is to live, think and work now for that which, in the tangible world, corresponds with the new picture in the ideal world. That is, while living in the subconscious expectation of a greater future, work for the realization of a greater now.

To constantly expect certain future realization is a part of life; the present is the cause, the future is the effect, and it is natural for the cause to look towards its own effect, but when the cause does not understand itself, it will picture the wrong effect; in consequence, it will misdirect its own forces and produce the wrong effect, because the life-forces will invariably create in the likeness of the pattern or picture that is provided by the mind.

This is the reason why man, through the misunderstanding of himself, has produced a future of age, weakness, decline, uselessness and emptyness, instead of a future of youth, vigor, health, power, attainment, happiness and worth. But by changing the picture of the coming years, he may cease to produce the former, and begin at once to produce the latter. To form the new picture, however, he must understand life as it is, and live, think and work accordingly.

The new picture of the coming years is based upon the principle that life, in personal form, can be perpetuated as long as the personal form is required for the advancement of the soul, and that this personal form may retain its youth as long as it continues to be.

To be true to the principle of life, is to picture such a future, and to live in the full subconscious expectation that every detail of that ideal picture will be realized. To live with such a future in view is to *think* that we are to be young always, that we are to grow in wisdom and power and love always, and that everything that a growing mind may desire will be added in greater and greater measure.

The new picture of the coming years pictures advancement in everything; health, vigor and youth at all times and under all circumstances; complete emancipation in the fullest and largest sense of that term; perpetual increase in personal capacity, mental power and intellectual brilliancy, constant improvement in all the elements of the personality, both as to form and expression; daily growth in wisdom, understanding, insight and realization; perpetual ascension into the higher realms of peace, harmony and joy; the steady development of a stronger and more beautiful character; the constant refinement of the entire human system; the growing interest in life, and everything that can add to the richness of life; the never ending betterment of friends, associations and environments; the daily advancement into new fields of life, thought, consciousness and action; the eternal ascension of the soul towards the supreme spiritual heights—the peace that passeth understanding, the joy everlasting and the infinite bliss of the cosmic state.

This is the new picture of the coming years— a picture that can be realized—a picture that *will* be realized by every individual who lives the ascending life, and who lives with this picture constantly in mind. To live for the realization of such a future, with the full subconscious expectation of such a future, is to create such a future. To live with such a future in the making—that, indeed, is *Life* and he who lives such a life will always stay young.

Printed in Great Britain
by Amazon.co.uk, Ltd.,
Marston Gate.